I want to read books by people who have lived compelling and nontraditional life stories. John and this book are paramount in this regard. The book is compelling and completely captivating not only because of John's life and stories but because the truths found therein are beyond powerful. This book has a surgeon's precision in diagnosing the problem but a surgeon's skill in the solution—it leaves you feeling healed and better than when you started it. Not many books do I buy a boxful to hand out, but this is one of them.

JEFFERSON BETHKE, *New York Times* bestselling author of *Jesus > Religion*

In *American Awakening*, John Kingston surveys an American landscape shot through with pessimism and partisanship, then offers hope. He charts a path to national renewal that doesn't depend on the outcome of the next election but rather on the remembering of ancient truths. His optimism about what this nation truly is and—just as importantly—can be bleeds through every page. *American Awakening* is a tonic for a troubled heart.

DAVID FRENCH, senior editor at the *Dispatch,* columnist for *Time*

A time of dreadful divisiveness requires the antidote of "radical togetherness"—a concept more rare and inspiring in practice than in theory. John Kingston takes us on his journey from wide-eyed student of Lincoln, King, and Mandela to faith-tested practitioner in the messy arena of civic life. Listen to his words because he's done the hard work of orienting his life and leading around these challenging ideas.

JOSH KWAN, president of The Gathering

*American Awakening* rings so powerfully true and is a must-read for all. The soul of America is more threatened now than at any time in modern history. This book not only offers a clarion call at the perfect pitch for a nation in trouble but also lays out a clear road map. The book reminds us that America's beginning and ending rest with "we the people." If we are to emerge from this challenging era as a better America, it will require each of us to become a better "me" and a better "we"!

REV. HURMON HAMILTON, senior and founding pastor
of New Beginnings Community Church

In a season where the forces of death, darkness, and division pillage the social fabric of our nation, John Kingston calls us to awaken to the life that is truly life. The timing for an American Awakening couldn't be better to give us vision to restore and rebuild.

GABE LYONS, president of Q Media, coauthor of *Good Faith*

Storytelling is one of the greatest gifts we can offer one another, and John masterfully tells the story of awakening and becoming, getting his hands dirty and doing good in a world that is so troubled. May we all learn to tell the truest truths so that we can build the kind of world we long to inhabit.

ROBYN HENDERSON-ESPINOZA, author of *Activist Theology*

John Kingston is a voice crying out in the wilderness. While so many Americans are afflicted by rampant depression, anxiety, and loneliness, *American Awakening* is Kingston's bold declaration of purpose, hope, and life. This is the book America most needs to read in 2020.

JEREMY COWART, photographer, founder of The Purpose Hotel

If you're tired of endless division, broken politics, and a society that seems to value all the wrong things, this is the book for you. By the time you finish the prologue, you'll already be more hopeful, but keep reading. John understands the fundamental brokenness that plagues our country—and hears the persistent heartbeat of a people yearning for something better.

ANDREW HANAUER, president and CEO of the One America Movement

John Kingston has issued a call to action, combining insights from an earnestly examined life with analysis from philosophical traditions and psychological research. He entertains, engages, informs, and inspires.

WALTER KIM, president of the National Association of Evangelicals

In an age when principles and virtues are shrouded by assumptions and distractions, John Kingston rises above the fray and offers a vision for awakening that honors the good of our past while offering hope to the weary in the present. I've listened, watched, and admired long enough to say with confidence that this man has a fervent pulse on the heartbeat of America—he too has won, lost, and arisen even stronger. Read his story and pay attention to your heart pounding within.

STEPHEN A. MACCHIA, founder and president of Leadership Transformations, author of more than a dozen books on spiritual transformation

This engaging, gripping book is at its core a call for renewal. It recognizes the problems confronting our society, but it also highlights our strengths and our capacity for social regeneration. The combination makes for just the kind of wake-up call America needs to hear.

YUVAL LEVIN, author of *A Time to Build*

"Radical togetherness" is not just a nice idea for John Kingston; it has been a lifelong pursuit. In strikingly insightful ways, John offers a profound and practical path forward amid the death and despair so many Americans are experiencing. *American Awakening* is for such a time as this!

REV. RAY HAMMOND

Radical togetherness is needed like never before. If Jesus's people can't do it, who can? I'm grateful for John's penning a great vision for awakening the soul of our country in a way that is beyond partisan politics. Both republicans and democrats promise the abundant life, but "all fall short of the glory of God." *American Awakening* is a call for Jesus's people of all varieties to find a life that is truly life. Read and join the adventure!

DAVID M. BAILEY, founder and director of Arrabon Enterprise Institute

John Kingston's deep love for his country, his passion to see people flourish, his penetrating insight into the state of the world, and his wisdom in human nature and the human predicament come through in brilliant colors. Underlying our social dysfunction, our political polarization, and the divisions along lines of ethnicity, class, and ideology is a far deeper problem. The roots that long nourished the American experiment have withered. Until we replenish those roots, there is no legislation and no political administration that can make us whole. Kingston is extraordinarily gifted at getting beyond the partisan warfare, the noise, and the statistics to the fundamental truths and values that ground us and hold us together as human beings and as Americans. I hope everyone reads this book. It would refresh and restrengthen the roots of our economy, our democracy, and our society.

TIMOTHY DALRYMPLE, president and CEO of *Christianity Today*

Our nation seems to face unprecedented challenges. If you are tempted to lose hope, read *American Awakening* by John Kingston. Without flinching from our national challenges, Kingston reminds us of the timeless truths about America that bind us together and make our country unique and great. This book gives the reader a much-needed shot of national confidence.

ARTHUR BROOKS, professor of the practice of public leadership, Harvard Kennedy School; senior fellow at Harvard Business School; president emeritus of the American Enterprise Institute

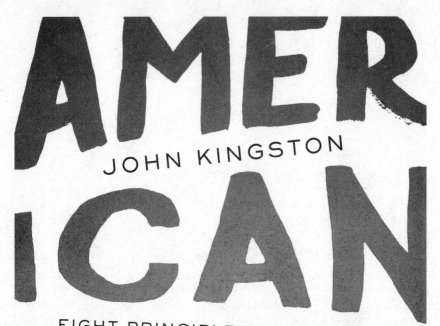

JOHN KINGSTON

EIGHT PRINCIPLES TO RESTORE

THE SOUL OF AMERICA

ZONDERVAN
BOOKS

ZONDERVAN BOOKS

*American Awakening*
Copyright © 2020 by John Kingston

Requests for information should be addressed to:
Zondervan, *3900 Sparks Dr. SE, Grand Rapids, Michigan 49546*

Zondervan titles may be purchased in bulk for educational, business, fundraising, or sales promotional use. For information, please email SpecialMarkets@Zondervan.com.

ISBN 978-0-310-36074-2 (hardcover)
ISBN 978-0-310-36076-6 (audio)
ISBN 978-0-310-36075-9 (ebook)

*Cover design: Lindy Martin / Faceout Studio*
*Cover illustration: Shutterstock / PyzhovaOlena / daniilphotos / Anastasiia Smiian*
*Interior design: Denise Froehlich*

*Printed in the United States of America*

20 21 22 23 24 / LSC / 10 9 8 7 6 5 4 3 2 1

*To my parents—and the parents of my wonderful Jean—*
*who did their very best to teach us these principles*

# CONTENTS

# FOREWORD

John Kingston loves America the way a twelve-year-old boy loves life. There's an eager hopefulness about him. There's a firm and earnest resolution to live up to the privilege of being an American. And above all there's a sense of mission, a conviction that this nation still has some great role to play in the great story of humanity and in God's providential design.

John not only loves America, he embodies America. He's the type, recognized the world over. And he is America right now. He maintains an ingrained bullishness toward the possibilities of tomorrow while realizing, as many of us do, that we've lost the thread. There's some social and spiritual malaise that threatens our self-confidence, our faith in the country and its institutions, and the answer is not seen in some return to a tainted past but still lies over the horizon, on the green breast of a new world.

John is American in the most obvious ways. He grew up in a working-class family, labored hard, was lucky enough to get into great schools, and made it into the ranks of the affluent through dogged effort and contribution. He has had a chance to live out Horatio Alger's dream.

But he's also American in a wider sense, the kind captured not merely in Alger's dream but in Ben Franklin's dream. And the watchword of the Franklin dream is *improvement*—daily, steady improvement. The goal of this dream is not to get rich but to be a better person in all ways. Franklin made a checklist of the virtues and resolved to work on embodying them a little more each day. Kingston's family has a mission statement. Franklin was an irrepressible learner and experimenter, and Kingston buckles down and reads everything that might help him see himself, our Maker, and our situation more clearly.

You'll know you're in the presence of a Franklin American when in the pages ahead he writes about his family vacations. Even they are structured to serve a purpose—family togetherness. Soccer turns out to be a game everyone can play with abandon, as one. A little improvement every day.

In America, at least in its best moments and places, personal transformation and social transformation happen at the same time. Franklin's personal improvement was indistinguishable from his civic improvement—founding libraries, fire departments, a great university, serving in public life. Kingston has led large online publications. He's experienced the thrill of running for public office and the agony of reading about it in the papers the next day.

And there's one more way John is quintessentially American. Deep down, America is not only a country, it's an eschatology. It's a dream that we represent the last best hope of humankind, that God's designs will be played out on these lands. This deep consciousness has always given Americans a certain future consciousness. We see the present from the vantage point of the future.

In pioneering days, the settlers would pass by really good farmland because they were sure something even better lay over the next hill. Waves of immigrants were willing to suffer the ordeal of uprooting themselves because they were already living, at least in their minds, in the glorious future that was to come. That same hungering for the future is on every page you're about to read.

But there's also an investigation into what's gone wrong—the way technology threatens our relationships, the way ease has led to self-indulgence, the way ongoing racial injustice has been a cancer eating away at flesh and bone.

This book exists because the old American narrative doesn't include all voices and is somehow no longer applicable today. This book exists because the traditional American consciousness that John embodies has to be remade. Not discarded. Remade.

John admits that he feels a bit lost. He bravely speaks for a lot of us. But this book is not about confusion. It's about the American consciousness trying to find its bigger next self.

And it is driven by an instinct for recovery: the way we remake our nation is in the warp and woof of everyday life. If we can find better ways to communicate with one another, redeem our moments of suffering, and greet our neighbors, then the net effect will be civic renewal. And so this is a book filled with wisdom reminding each of us how to lead a better life right now. Individual advancement will serve the common good; the *imago Dei* imprinted on each human being will be recognized and poured out for a cause greater than self. Our national culture at its best has always been about the dance between the health of the individual and that of the community. John is simply choreographing it for a new era.

There's a moment in the pages ahead in which one of John's sons is in a period of confusion and finds clarity by going on a wilderness adventure. Hardship, challenge, and simplicity in the woods. If there's an antidote that runs more clearly through American history, we don't know what it is. The true sources of our wealth are not stockpiled in the banks or in our most civilized parts but in our nature, in simplicity, in the original gifts God gave us, in how we struggle against and with one another.

It's possible that America is in decline. We had our moment and it's time for China or somebody else to take the lead. But this book is a reminder that America is not merely a GDP but a way of being, and the instincts and belief we hold in common are still there, if we'd just remember our younger hope and apply it to the challenges at hand.

DAVID BROOKS AND ANNE SNYDER

# RESTORING THE SOUL OF AMERICA

I never saw my dad drink a drop of alcohol.

My family members, fundamentalist Christians, were deeply opposed to the bottle. I was raised to believe that teetotaling was the only proper path. But Dad slurred his words a lot of evenings and behaved in ways that just seemed weird.

Maybe I shouldn't have been shocked when my mother announced that Dad was headed to rehab when I was seventeen years old, but I was.

I'd swallowed the "religion" thing whole, attending church every Sunday morning and night, every Wednesday night for prayer meeting, and every Friday night for youth group, as the evil in the world "out there" was renounced. But the moment I heard my mother's news, I realized that the darkness of deceit, lies, and escapism had lurked in our own home. In my own father. Maybe even in me?

We joined my dad for a week at the rehab center as a family exercise. While the rehab center was fine by 1983 standards, for this high school senior, the whole experience prompted more questions than answers.

There I was educated on the psychology of birth order in families of addiction. As much as I hated to admit it, I was a poster child for the oldest sibling. Suddenly, I wondered whether my goal-oriented perfectionism was just a twist of fate. Did I even have choices?

The experience shook me to my core. Even though I'd believed that getting into an Ivy League school was a major achievement, it suddenly felt hollow. It now seemed I was fated for that path, programmed by my birth order to do nothing other than achieve. While an Ivy League education was a huge opportunity for a working-class kid, I decided I couldn't take advantage of it without knowing who I truly was.

Way before anyone talked about taking a gap year between high school and college, I decided not to enroll for classes at the University of Pennsylvania. Instead, I bought a bus ticket and headed out onto the highways. Before the age of cell phones, the internet, and constant communication, I put my savings—a little over $1,000—into my pocket and boarded a Greyhound. I didn't care where it took me. I just needed to go.

I was gone for nine months and traversed ten thousand miles via bus and hitchhiking, living on five dollars a day. Even those words—*bus* and *hitchhiking*—seem outdated in an era of Uber and hypervigilance.

But I'm not interested in a call back to a hazy goodness of the past that never really existed (especially since those "good old days" like the 1950s were rarely good for marginalized Americans). In the pages to come, I'd like to evoke principles older than those seen on *Happy Days* and *I Love Lucy* and more enduring than those in *This Is Us*. While I'll recall the evidence of our shared values in the music, sports, and other events we celebrate together, I'd like to ultimately highlight the common principles that have animated the greatest traditions and societies in history—from ancient Greece to remote tribes to modern America—principles that can still empower us beyond our differences today. Coupled with new scientific findings and undeniable social progress in some areas, these principles can change your life and mine. They might even change the world.

But I'm getting ahead of myself.

When I lived in my small town, I dreamed of the great vistas of America, principally through my passion for sports, movies, books, and music. I would watch whatever sports were on the networks and read whatever book or article I could; through them I'd dream of the worlds my heroes inhabited. The great Walt "Clyde" Frazier was one of the earliest trendsetting superstars. He wore fur coats and drove Rolls-Royces and won NBA championships with the New York Knicks. Clyde's beautiful game and cosmopolitan life transported me to the world of New York City, as did *Heaven Is a Playground*, Rick Telander's journalistic masterpiece describing the city's urban playgrounds where some of basketball's legends came from and where could-have-been legends fell prey to the ravages of the streets.

With my own pop-culture montage reeling in my head, I set off to see this great country I dreamed of to find what was real "out there" and to discover what was real about me.

Only seventeen and on the road alone, I dipped a toe in the Atlantic and headed west toward the Pacific. I experienced the grandeur of our national monuments in Washington, DC, the neon electricity of Manhattan, the cobblestone history of Philadelphia, the down-home goodness of the heartland, and the "new world" promise of California. I found along the way the playgrounds that were heavens and the great American fields of dreams. With the soundtrack of America ringing in my ears, I played ball on Manhattan's famous Fourth Street courts and sought out the Bronx of Grandmaster Flash and the Furious Five, trying to breathe in the line: "It's like a jungle sometimes. It makes me wonder how I keep from going under." I visited the rock quarries of Bloomington, Indiana, where the cutters of the film *Breaking Away* swam, and then I secretly slept at half-court in Indiana University's renowned Assembly Hall. I woke up wanting to "sweat it out on the streets of a runaway American dream" with Bruce Springsteen. I naively tried to look "back on when I was a little nappy-headed boy" with Stevie Wonder and understand "what's going on" with Marvin Gaye, while receiving a daily education, including losing my two front teeth on the magical Venice Beach basketball courts in Los Angeles. As I traveled to each new place, I continued "calling out in transit" with R.E.M. and wondering "how does it feel to be on your own?" with Bob Dylan.

I never once paid for accommodations. I stayed in men's shelters, in parks, on a bench outside the Smithsonian, and on the couches of amazing and generous people I met. My up-close encounter with this great, complicated country started a head-over-heels love affair.

I saw that America, in all its complexity, is magnificent and majestic, as well as charming and mysterious. It is filled with wonderful and broken people just like me, people of every skin color, young and old, rich and poor, with ideals spanning from the most liberal socialism to the most ardent conservativism. And while our dreams are as diverse as our personal experiences, we remain bonded over our deepest hopes and longings.

In discovering this, I mysteriously began to discover myself. I began to see a place for me in this wide world—as a unique individual with something to offer and as a vibrant thread woven into the huge, rich tapestry of humanity.

Much has changed about America, and me, since that 1980s journey.

The nation I used to know has morphed into something that would've been unrecognizable to me back in the era of Ronald Reagan's optimism and the curious clarity of having seemingly only one adversary in the world (the Soviet Union, of course) in the Cold War.*

As I finalize this book for publication, our nation and the world are in the early throes of the COVID-19 pandemic. The implications of the pandemic—medically, psychologically, economically, and in our culture and patterns of life going forward—are uncertain and will remain so for some time.

And yet even ahead of this time, despair, division, and death have been on the march in our land. There were 150,000 deaths of despair (suicide, drug overdose, and alcohol-related deaths) in the US last year alone. When we aren't killing ourselves, we are killing each other in tragic ways. One recent twenty-four-hour period sadly illustrates this. On the morning of August 3, 2019, a gunman opened fire in a crowded shopping center in El Paso, Texas, killing twenty-two people and injuring twenty-four more.

---

* I know it was actually more complicated than this, but there is something to the fact that the threats were clearer because they could be identified as from the outside, rather than today's "threats," which so often seem to come from within.

Thirteen hours later and 1,600 miles away, another gunman opened fire on a crowd outside a bar in Dayton, Ohio, killing nine people and leaving twenty-seven injured.[1] While these men had nearly opposite views of the societal ills motivating them to lash out in such violent ways (not that any social problem can be reasonably seen as such motivation, of course), they seemingly shared the same psychological afflictions.

While thanks be to God that the great majority of us don't feel so afflicted as to be suicidal or criminally pathological, in every demographic, we feel more anxious, depressed, lonely, alienated, and divided than ever before. As a nation, even ahead of the COVID-19 pandemic, we may have never felt so hostage to fear and pain. And now it seems there's no end in sight. Unless there is a dramatic departure from recent patterns, the 2020 election cycle is likely to lengthen the shadow of despair and division, no matter who wins. Indeed, if the recent past is any indication, political leaders may offer "solutions" that not only will fail to heal our brokenness but may finally split us wide open.

Rarely have we felt so pitted against one another—on matters big and small.

The great American experiment seems to be failing.

I've felt this cultural angst myself, in my own family and with my own friends. We have dealt with addiction, depression, and anxiety, losing loved ones to their battles, which makes us like just about everybody. I've found myself having conversations I never anticipated when I was growing up—negotiating the consequences of severe addictions and selfish decisions and the backlash of damaged relationships.

Perhaps like you, I have continued trying to locate myself, my story, and my potential contributions across the full range of the American experience. After my cross-country journey for the better part of a year, I did move from my working-class background to an Ivy League school, followed by an Ivy League law school. At Penn, I met my future wife, Jean, a wonderful woman born into a family of Chinese-American immigrants. I also joined Penn's gospel choir as the only white guy among the seventy-five or so members. I then pledged Alpha Phi Alpha, the first fraternity for African American men, where Martin Luther King Jr., Jesse Owens, and many other American heroes pledged and where I was once again the only white member. Far from my fundamentalist church upbringings, I looked for fellowship and community in evangelical, Lutheran, African-Methodist Episcopal, Church of God in Christ, Roman Catholic, Anglo-Catholic, Presbyterian, Episcopalian, Vineyard, Baptist, Pentecostal, and Charismatic churches, and even across Jewish and Muslim divides.

I made the most of the stepping-stones created by my Penn and Harvard degrees; my business career brought me more wealth, prosperity, and status than I had ever dreamed possible. Because I love America and all the benefits it has afforded me, I've tried to give back. I've spent millions to create organizations that support our military members and their families, to partner with organizations that provide "ladder of success" opportunities for those who have been left behind, and to build organizations focused on intergenerational virtue transfer. I helped create one of the world's largest religious and faith-oriented websites, and I've worked with teams to make films, some of them even successful.*

Most recently, I ran for the United States Senate in the great commonwealth of Massachusetts.

I lost.

And in a way, I feel lost again, and as unsettled as ever before. As I have seen in speaking with thousands of people at hundreds of events over the last three years, this feeling makes me like so many fellow citizens in my state and our country.

Now I find myself realizing that perhaps there's nothing I can offer to our nation other than my desperate desire for things to work out and

---

* If you are curious, these aren't the kind of films that open on thousands of screens and in a theater near you, but rather smaller-budget films in the independent film world. This includes a number of different narrative feature films (*And Then I Go* [2017]) and *This Is the Year* [expected 2020 release]), as well as documentary efforts (*The Game Changers* [2018], *More Art Upstairs* [2017], and an upcoming documentary on Henri Nouwen [expected 2020 release]). The most successful was 2014's *Mitt*, which had the prime opening slot at Sundance Film Festival and was one of Netflix's first original content offerings.

for our country to live up to its possibility and potential. While I care deeply for every nation, America is the only place I live. It is the only place I can touch every day. But truth be told, the world is better when America is strong. Really, the world can't have peace and prosperity if America is wobbling on internal polarization and insecurity.

Deep down, I hope that somehow, together, we can restore what's been lost in our collective national soul.

We won't find healing in Washington or through the institutions and powers of this world. Though we feel ill-equipped for the moment, we have to rise together, or we will fall apart. The world is depending on us. We are depending on us. The good news is that if our history is any clue, we can and will figure out our cultural challenges, and we will be okay. We can and will get this right. As long as "we" do this *together.*

In preparing this book, I worked with an array of collaborators and research assistants to review the insights of the principal ancient and contemporary systems of thought, from the major Eastern and Western philosophical traditions and major religions to the positive psychologists and the most current popular and academic books. I also worked with social scientists and neuroscientists at Harvard and Ohio State to bring you the best current scientific thinking.

In short, I have done the work of synthesizing the insights of the ages and contemporary science so you don't have to.

Now and then I will offer my perspective on these matters from my Judeo-Christian vantage point, but generally the material rests on a broader foundation, integrating all the threads we find through history. This book is for everyone, and you don't need to share my faith to benefit from our discoveries.

Depending on your point of view, you may be surprised to learn I have found that all our work points to the following general statement: We were each put here on earth with a special purpose and role to be found in our own place and time, through faith in something greater than ourselves, commitment to family, and contribution to the community (directly or indirectly through the work we do).

To break this down a bit further, I have found eight principles that have withstood the test of time and will help us restore the soul of America. I wrestled with the idea of adapting this book to be more "current" given the immediate coronavirus crisis, but as I thought further about it, there was little of importance to be added. These are "forever" principles, our need to recall them has become even clearer, and the time to share them is now. Amid the challenges of this moment—including the effects of COVID-19—these principles remain timeless:

1. You Have a Purpose: Believe It
2. You Long for Renewal: Find More in Less
3. You Will Face Adversity: Redeem It
4. You Need People: Engage in Person
5. You Are Not Alone: Share Your Highs and Lows
6. We Are More Alike than Different: Respond Instead of React
7. I Am You Are We: There Is No Them, There Is Only Us
8. Together We Will Awaken America: Fulfilling Our Promise

Though the days are indeed dark, the opportunity for an awakening is great; it can start here and now and bring us to a new understanding and experience of life, that is, living as we were truly meant to live—individually empowered, collectively strengthened. This begins when we realize we don't *have* to serve one another or a greater good; we *get* to do so, and in doing so we will *all* receive what we are looking for.

We won't embrace these principles because we *should* embrace them. As many experience in hastily beating a retreat from their New Year's resolutions, it is hardly ever sustainable to do what we "should" do.

My hope is that because these principles describe who we are as individuals, and who we are meant to be together, we will *want* to embrace them, because they will provide us the freedom to experience a life that is truly life.

# CHAPTER 1

# WE NEED TO REMEMBER

## THE COST OF FORGETTING

Sometimes, as a culture, we forget.

The Romans came up with the perfect recipe for making concrete that enabled them to construct magnificent structures that have stood the test of time.[1] The Colosseum might look a little run-down, but you can forgive some of the deterioration when you realize the structure is almost two thousand years old. This concrete allowed builders to make beautiful homes that would impress even modern eyes. And the stunning remains of some of these structures still dot the Mediterranean landscape, including the Pantheon and Trajan's Market.

Then something happened.

The Romans lost the recipe.

Why it wasn't passed down from one generation to the next remains a mystery. Some speculate that the concrete recipe was a highly guarded trade secret, known only to stonemasons who died without passing down their knowledge. Others speculate the loss of the recipe was merely a mistake.

Whatever the case, the Romans somehow lost their ability to make the magic concrete, and they found themselves living in homes they no longer knew how to build. Though they enjoyed the benefits of houses built by their ancestors, their modern lives were precariously dependent on a successful recipe they could no longer re-create.

In America, we are in a similar place. Chances are, if you picked up this book, you don't need to be convinced of how bad things have gotten in this country. You might have experienced—in yourself or your family—some of the many afflictions that plague our modern age: depression, addiction, abuse, or even suicide. You might even find yourself puzzled when you witness the inherent contradictions of modern life.

**We are more connected than ever, but we're still lonely.**

According to a recent report from health insurance giant Cigna (with data generated ahead of the coronavirus crisis), almost half of Americans report sometimes or always feeling alone or left out. One in four rarely or never feel as though people really understand them. Two in five sometimes or always feel that their relationships aren't meaningful and that they are isolated from others. One in five people report that they rarely or never feel close to people or feel like there are people they can talk to.[2]

Only half of us report having meaningful in-person social interactions on a daily basis.

Young adults (ages eighteen to twenty-two years old) report being the loneliest generation. This is surprising, especially for those of us who are far from the prime of our youth. They even claim to be in worse health than their older counterparts. Though it would be easy to blame this loneliness on the rise of social media, Cigna respondents who use social media all the time reported about the same level of loneliness of those who never do.

**We have more access to healthier food, but we're more obese.**

Since there are a number of trendy diets, we can choose our specific diet strategy: carb cycling, paleo, intermittent fasting, ketogenic, Miami Beach, alkaline (also known as the Tom Brady diet). And most stores have plenty of healthy food options—from organic to "locavore" to vegan selections—but we're fatter than ever.

In addition to facing a loneliness epidemic, we're also in the throes of an obesity epidemic. Global obesity has nearly tripled since 1975. And of the people born between 1981 and 1996, 70 percent will be obese by the time they reach middle age.[3] This means that obesity-related diseases like diabetes, heart disease, and cancer will increase dramatically. New York University's Marion Nestle, former chair of the department of nutrition and food studies, predicts that the costs of obesity-related illnesses will be "astronomical" in the future.[4] The number of diabetes patients alone might increase enough to "break the bank of our healthcare system," according to the director of the Center for Human Nutrition, Dr. James O. Hill.[5]

**We have unimaginable wealth, but we think we're poor.**

In March 2019, *Time* magazine's Charlotte Alter wrote a cover article on the youngest member of Congress. To promote it, the journalist tweeted that she and the congressmember—who were born the same year—had the same challenging economic experiences. "She was a Dunkaroos kid—I liked fruit roll-ups. People our age have never experienced American prosperity in our adult lives—which is why so many millennials are embracing Democratic socialism."

Her tweet caused many people to immediately google "What are Dunkaroos and Fruit Roll-Ups?" (To save you the trouble, they are both snack foods that the reporter believed helpfully designated people below thirty.) Her tweet also caused many to scratch their heads in disbelief.

Though no nation or economic system is perfect, America has provided so much wealth, stability, and prosperity that people who grew up eating Dunkaroos are some of the richest, safest, and most privileged people ever to walk this planet. In the past decade, ahead of the coronavirus recession, this generation had known only steady economic growth, and unemployment rates were lower than any in recorded history. And the affordability of near-miracle products and services? Astounding. From inexpensive smartphones with remarkable functions (thank you, Samsung and Apple) to car services that arrive at the push of a button (looking at you, Uber and Lyft) to *free* navigation services around the planet (Waze and Google Maps), we all get so much more for our money now. As one observer noted, "Working adults before the 2000s understand how difficult it would be, for instance, to separately buy all the functions available on a simple smartphone. Wages have also grown . . .

living standards have increased. Put this way, millennials live better than John D. Rockefeller."[6]

**We have an increasingly pain-free existence, but we're medicating ourselves to death.**

Holding aside the coronavirus pandemic, we live in a time of relative ease, where modern conveniences isolate us from the hardship of manual labor and diplomacy from the necessity of combat. Yet in spite of our peace and prosperity, we're accidentally killing ourselves with drugs and alcohol at an unprecedented rate.

According to the Centers for Disease Control and Prevention, over 770,000 people died from a drug overdose from 1999 to 2018.

In 2018 alone, 67,400 people overdosed; around 68 percent of those deaths involved an opioid—that's six times the number of death-by-opioid than occurred in 1999.[7]

Excessive alcohol use is responsible for about 88,000 deaths a year, including one in ten total deaths among working-age adults ages twenty to sixty-four years.[8] This tragic trend shows little sign of abating.

**We have comfortable lives, but we're ending them prematurely.**

Too frequently we turn on the news or check our Twitter feeds and see that another high-profile person has taken his or her own life: from Kate Spade to Anthony Bourdain to Robin Williams and so many others. Suicide is at a fifty-year peak. The Centers for Disease Control and Prevention released a study in 2016 revealing that suicide rates in the United States have risen nearly 30 percent since 1999.[9] Since 2008, suicide was the tenth leading cause of death for all ages.[10] In 2016 suicide became the second leading cause of death for ages ten to thirty-four and the fourth leading cause for ages thirty-five to fifty-four.[11] In the United States between 2007 and 2015, the number of children and teens who experienced suicidal thoughts and suicide attempts so strongly that they visited the emergency room doubled.[12] (Imagine how many didn't go to the hospital.)

Nearly 150,000 suicides and drug- and alcohol-related deaths occur

per year—an unprecedented and staggering number—and as a consequence, American life expectancy fell three of the past four years before
COVID-19.

**Deaths of despair climbing at a staggering rate.**

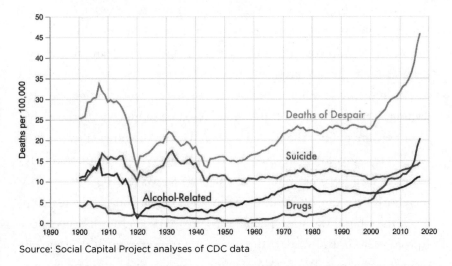

Source: Social Capital Project analyses of CDC data

### We're more educated, but we know less.

Today we take for granted technological advancement that would've
stunned our predecessors. Compared with them, we are godlike in our
immediate access to information. Also, more people are going to college
than ever before in American history. In 1965, 5.9 million Americans
enrolled in college. In 2018, that number was 20 million.[13] Now almost
90 percent of students attend college within eight years of high school
graduation, despite the skyrocketing cost of education.[14]

But even with all this education and access to information, we have
less knowledge and seem to lack the basic reasoning skills of our predecessors. In fact, we're in the middle of what some people have called a
"disinformation age."

Stanford historian Robert Proctor even created the term *agnotology*,
derived from the Greek word *agnosis*, to describe "the study of cultur-
ally constructed ignorance." He believes that ignorance is increasing,

especially surrounding hot-button topics, because so many people are purposefully spreading incorrect information to suppress truth.[15] That may very well be true, but it's not hard to mislead people who are willing to be misled.

I'm sure you've seen one late-night talk show send someone out into the streets of New York to ask basic questions to pedestrians. Jimmy Kimmel most recently perfected the art of asking basic questions—about the world or government—only to reveal that people can't name their congressman, the vice president, or whether or not the president released his tax returns. Though the idiot-on-the-streets schtick might be misleading, it might be funnier if it didn't resonate so much with the reality of our failing public schools and general decline of knowledge.

We not only know less, we think less sharply. An examination of IQ scores of men born between 1962 and 1991 shows that IQ increased for men born between 1962 and 1975, but then began a steady decrease.[16]

If the biblical warning "people are destroyed from lack of knowledge" is true, we're in bad shape.[17] Because we've forgotten more than just the recipe for concrete. We've forgotten the basic principles of sound living.

We live in a culture that still benefits from the wisdom of those who went before us, and yet we are flailing and seemingly failing today because we've forgotten the recipe.

But there is a solution.

Over the course of history, scientists have tried to re-create the lost recipe of Roman concrete, and rumors abounded. Ancient builders in China added sticky rice to their concrete because they believed their staple food would make it stronger. Did the Romans include unexpected ingredients like milk? Blood? The knowledge was lost. The modern cement you can buy at a hardware store today—though strong and inexpensive—crumbles after several years. But what was it about the Roman concrete that allowed structures like the Colosseum to exist with so little maintenance?

University of Utah geology professor Marie Jackson tried to get to the bottom of this mystery. She read Pliny the Elder's *Naturalis Historia* from AD 77, a work that attempted to describe all human knowledge and is one of the largest and most expansive works to survive from the Roman world. Right there, in Latin, Pliny the Elder described how they created a material "that as soon as it comes into contact with the waves of the sea and is submerged becomes a single stone mass, impregnable to the waves and every day stronger."[18]

Immediately, Jackson and her team examined the many Roman ports in Italy and confirmed that this ancient text was, in fact, correct. "Long-term chemical resilience of the concrete evidently relied on water-rock interactions, as Pliny the Elder inferred."

They also found a rare mineral: aluminous tobermorite. Most modern laboratories can't even produce this mineral since it's "formed in lime particles through pozzolanic reaction at somewhat elevated temperatures."[19] In other words: in volcanoes. By mixing volcanic sand, pumice, and lime with mortar, the Romans created a "hydraulic concrete," which was able to withstand brutal forces of weather and time. Their material was able to expand in ways that modern concrete can't. The volcanic material, as Jackson explained, "was the secret to concretes that were very well bonded, coherent, robust materials" that provided unprecedented strength and hardiness.

Hardiness seems almost old-fashioned in the modern world of trigger warnings, microaggressions, and the highly offended. However, that's mainly because we've either never known or can't remember the original recipe that built our resoluteness in the first place.

Even in America's abundance, we search for the ingredients that can create lives that are well-bonded, coherent, and robust. It's my contention that to re-create this more stable foundation, we must look to the people who came before us. I don't want to be part of a generation guilty of not passing down the recipe for abundant living. Like you, I want to discover a renewed understanding and experience of life far greater than our ancestors envisioned. Though this will require deliberately challenging some of today's cultural norms, the principles that can lead us to this experience are available and applicable right now—perhaps more than they've ever been. And the results, like the ancient Roman concrete, are both immediate and enduring.

The question you and I should ask ourselves is this: Does my approach to life track with these principles? If my answer or yours is no to any one of them, then our steps to a better life, and a better world, are clear. I have faith that enough of us will take them.

# PART 1

# CHAPTER 2

# YOU HAVE A PURPOSE

## BELIEVE IT

*W*e hold these truths to be self-evident, that all men are created equal, that they are endowed by their Creator with certain unalienable Rights, that among these are Life, Liberty and the pursuit of Happiness.[1]

You could make a compelling argument that this statement—famously written by Thomas Jefferson in the Declaration of Independence in 1776—is one of the top five most influential sentences of all time. This line helped launch the greatest social experiment ever known—self-government in a democratic republic. And hundreds of years later, this radical experiment has been successful enough that it has been followed by many nations around the world.*

If you think all the way back to your high school history classes (but who remembers those, right?), you may recall that until the final drafting stages, Jefferson described the key unalienable rights as "Life, Liberty and Property." The concept of the right of "property" was in line with more conventional understandings of many of the intellectual giants Jefferson followed. This shows us how much a single word can change the target we aim for. As an illustration, consider if Jesus had said in the Sermon on

---

*  Without delving too deeply into this point, we certainly must acknowledge that it has taken hundreds of years and great suffering and bloodshed for the key principle "all are created equal" to be experienced more broadly. The process for this to be achieved across color and gender lines continues, and the principle remains an aspiration yet to be fully realized.

the Mount, "Blessed are the super powerful," instead of "Blessed are the meek."[2] That would have changed a lot, right?

What if I were to tell you that the word *happiness* as used by Jefferson was about as different from our 2020 concept of happiness as the concept of property is from happiness? This profound phrase—"Life, Liberty and the Pursuit of Happiness"—has deeply influenced us, and yet we are thinking about something utterly different than what was intended.

I don't want to make your eyes glaze over with references to ancient Greek and Roman and seventeenth-century Enlightenment philosophers, but play along with me for just a minute. (I'm suddenly reminded of *The Princess Bride*, when Inigo Montoya says, "Let me explain. No, not enough time, let me sum up.") I promise I won't use Greek and Latin words throughout the book, but please indulge me with this one. *Eudaimonia* is the word Aristotle used in his masterwork to describe the condition of human flourishing, or of living well.* The unfortunate part is that the standard English translation of this Greek word is "happiness," which in the modern understanding means "state of mind or feeling of pleasure/contentment." This definition couldn't be further afield from the meaning of *eudaimonia* that Aristotle and other ancients understood. According to Aristotle, every living or human-made thing has a unique function that distinguishes it from all other things, and the highest good of that thing consists of the good performance of its function. If it is a table, then the characteristics are "having a flat and level plane" and "holding objects"—and the highest good of that table is when it is, you guessed it, being flat and holding objects.

Sounds a lot like the purpose of that table, right? This notion of performing your highest function is how Aristotle defined happiness: doing whatever it is you were made to do.

Back to Jefferson. He described happiness in a similar sense. He drew on the ancients like Aristotle and also the Enlightenment thinkers like

---

* Aristotle, *Nicomachean Ethics*—I wonder whether many of you, like me, don't remember much from our high school philosophy classes.

John Locke, who discussed the "pursuit of true and solid happiness," warning that we "mistake not imaginary for real happiness."[3]

As we will see in this chapter, from Aristotle to the Stoics, Epicureans, Enlightenment thinkers, and our Declaration, the understanding of finding happiness was rooted in who and what you were made to be.

Or as I would summarize it—you were made for the pursuit of your purpose.

Like any normal human being, and maybe especially any red-blooded American, I enjoy a virtually endless list of pleasures:

- a comfortable bed
- working out—a good basketball game or soccer match best of all (when I was a younger man)
- date nights with my wonderful wife
- SkinnyPop Popcorn

I could go on and on, but you get the idea.

There is nothing wrong with pleasure or comfort; we are wired for it, and it is as natural as can be. But the problem for so many of us (myself included) is that when we think of the "pursuit of happiness" in the modern age, we can't help but think of the individual search for pleasure or comfort. The paradox is that the focused search for individual pleasure and comfort will never help you achieve the happiness you truly desire. As great philosopher and economist John Stuart Mill observed, happiness will come as the unintended outcome of aiming at something else.[4] Or as amusing British writer and social observer Ruth Whippman noted in her aptly titled *America the Anxious*, "Like an attractive man, it seems the more actively happiness is pursued, the more it refuses to call and starts avoiding you at parties."[5]

I started this book by telling you about one wilderness adventure, when my life seemed to have turned upside down at seventeen and I hit the American roads for the better part of a year. While I had my normal share of ups and downs from there, many years later I arrived at another wilderness moment.

As I have shared, I grew up in a working-class community and didn't grow up with any real expectation of wealth. After some interesting twists and turns in the law and business worlds, I ended up with a wonderful set of business partners at a publicly traded investment management company, Affiliated Managers Group (more often described as AMG).* During the period I served with the AMG management team, we grew from a market enterprise value of $100 million to nearly $15 billion, managing over $600 billion of assets at the time of my departure. My business career brought me more wealth and opportunity than I had ever dreamed possible. When I was growing up in a working-class town, and even in my college, law school, and earliest professional years, I never really thought about or aimed for financial success. Instead, I always thought about my duty and the mission I was on at any given time—and occasionally thought about my broader mission beyond the immediate (or calling, as it is at times described).

Just ahead of my joining AMG in 1999, I sat down with my wife, Jean, to write a family mission statement. (You can see the full text of it on page 46, in the form in which it has been on the family kitchen bulletin board for a very long time.) I was in a much different stage of life; I was still a relatively young professional, had two children (with a third on the way), and, like so many, was under a mountain of student loan debt. Like a lot of young husbands and fathers and professionals, I felt a great deal of personal uncertainty about my direction and my roles in the

---

\* While I would love to give shout-outs to so many of my wonderful colleagues and friends at AMG, I will especially mention my two bosses during my period there, Sean Healey and Nate Dalton. Sean (longtime chairman and CEO) and Nate (who took a shot in hiring me as a young man and succeeded Sean as CEO) taught me great lessons, and I was honored to work alongside them in building a remarkable business.

world. Against that uncertainty, our mission statement was my effort to articulate the key principles I wanted to live by.

As I look back many years later, I am struck by two things. One is a great surprise to me—I am a guy who *always* looks at words I have written and tries to improve them, and yet curiously, all these years later, the mission statement is in exactly the same form in which I drafted it as a young man. It contains the same principles and the same statement—I haven't changed and wouldn't change a thing! The second is how little the "younger me" seemed to care about outcomes (at least on paper!) but rather only what our aspirations or approaches should be. So this mission wasn't about *what* we would do, but instead *who we were as people* and *how we should approach life.*

At the outset of the statement, we made these commitments:

Our Mission is to live every day and every experience passionately and fully in a fashion pleasing to our Heavenly Father.

We believe that our Father loves his children completely and without condition, and has a special role and place for each child.

In our home we will show each of God's children—both inside our family and out—that love, and encourage each to find his or her special role and place.

For many years I knew I was to apply these commitments in the workplace by honoring my bosses, teammates, partners, and the shareholders of the company, helping them achieve what they were put on this planet to do. I primarily thought about how I was supposed to apply myself daily, do the best work I could do, and achieve the job I was asked to achieve.

Since I always had a strong sense of mission even beyond the office, in my spare time I routinely found something new to create or a meaningful partnership to build. That sense of mission and duty to do something to improve our community, state, nation, or world manifested itself in a drive that I couldn't turn off.

Given that my wife's and my anchoring commitment was to help others in their role and place, this expressed itself in my helping remarkable people do the work they were already doing. I would find great men and women working to change the world (in Boston, Massachusetts, America, or beyond) and do all I could do with my limited spare time to advance them in their missions. You might see a pattern here; this was similar to my daily mission at AMG, where I helped great men and women in their missions in the finance world.

To give some examples, two of the earliest partnerships during those years were with two great Boston families, that of Reverend Hurmon Hamilton, then a minister at Boston's Roxbury Presbyterian Church, and Governor (and later presidential candidate) Mitt Romney. Both men and their families are driven by great vision and a profound sense of duty, and I felt strongly that it was my mission to help them wherever possible.

It would take another book to share Hurmon's amazing life story. Here is a one-sentence version: with the assistance of the great love and commitment of the Louisiana great-aunt who raised him, Hurmon over-came the scarring and partial blindness that resulted from a tragic medical misstep when he was an infant to become a tremendous visionary leader. Trying to make the most of my then-limited hours, I leaned in to help Hurmon in any way possible, underwriting new project management initiatives and galvanizing financial support for his efforts.*

My efforts with the Romneys started humbly when I was still a young professional at AMG (nearly twenty years ago now!), hosting fundraisers for him and his lieutenant governor candidate, Kerry Healey.† As the years went by and Governor Romney considered a presidential run, I

---

* Perhaps our most noteworthy partnership in those early years was one to help get the Hamilton family out of Roxbury when his adolescent son was threatened by encroaching gang violence on the very street the Hamiltons lived on. I clearly remember the moment Hurmon shared the story of his pain and fear for his family; I was driving through my town center and pulled over to the side of the road to form a plan to help him solve this tremendous challenge. That day, Hurmon and I formed a business partnership to buy a home for the Hamiltons outside the city, providing refuge for their son and much-needed peace of mind for Hurmon and his wife, Rhonda.

† Kerry was at that time the wife of my AMG boss, Sean Healey—small world!

pulled together a team from across the country to advance grassroots initiatives (and later media-driven initiatives) for the Romney family and team. Perhaps our most memorable outing was at the 2006 Southern Republican Leadership Conference. With my wonderful teammates, I helped deliver a very surprising second-place SRLC straw poll finish that made for great "Massachusetts Mitt delivers in Memphis" headlines for a couple of cycles.*

Eventually, I felt my focus shifting and my mission moving away from my business life at AMG to supporting great men and women and projects shaping and improving the world. I left AMG at the beginning of 2015 and doubled down on a variety of partnerships and projects that I had started working on through the years. Though the objectives and details varied, they were all connected by one theme: each of God's children matters and should be encouraged in his or her unique place on the planet.

I was always interested in promoting freedom of speech and freedom of religion generally and in shaping the minds and hearts of later generations, and I worked on a number of efforts to that end. In the campus world, I helped start the Veritas Forum, founded at Harvard in 1992; the Society for Law, Life and Religion, founded at Harvard Law School in 1993; and Veritas Riff, founded in 2010. I continued working in this arena, continuing my board work with Veritas and advancing freedom of speech and thought on campuses with the Foundation for Excellence in Higher Education and Harvard's Human Flourishing Program.† Through these projects, I collaborated with some of the world's most

---

*    Numbered among the wonderful teammates were David and Nancy French, who are each accomplished writers and thought leaders. Full disclosure: Nancy provided some wonderful contributions to this book; thank you, Nancy! And if you aren't familiar with David's work, you should check out his regular contributions to *Time* magazine and the *Dispatch*, and look for his next book to be released in 2020, *Divided We Fall: America's Secession Threat and How to Restore Our Nation*.

†    The work of Dr. Tyler VanderWeele and Dr. Matthew Lee of the Human Flourishing Program was very helpful to us in developing this book—thank you, Tyler and Matt.

brilliant academics, working to advance their ideas in the most critical marketplace of ideas—college campuses.

We started a family project called SixSeeds (named after our six family members), designed to help parents instill principles of character formation in the next generation. We originally launched with a pilot project with World Vision in which we took families with very young family members (two to four years old) to work and play alongside and build relationships with local communities abroad.

My youngest son, William, playing soccer with
some boys in Tijuana, Mexico, in 2008.

Over time, the SixSeeds initiative became an online magazine, and we partnered with Patheos, a sizable faith-based website, to advance our reach to families. As the partnership evolved, I eventually became the principal owner of Patheos (at one point the world's largest multi-faith website), and then we merged the Patheos and Beliefnet companies (Beliefnet being another very large religious website).

I partnered with some of the nation's greatest think tanks and public policy initiatives, serving in various capacities with the American Enterprise Institute, Pioneer Institute, and Campaign to Fix the Debt (now Fix the Debt) to address the most pressing of our public policy problems. I worked with political candidates and elected officials to try to advance what I believed to be the best policy initiatives for the good of all citizens.

As I mentioned before, I had made some movies, and so I worked to create additional partnerships to make more movies because I wanted to tell stories that would encourage and motivate and inspire. To develop the strongest possible storytelling capacities, I invested in and partnered with world-class digital creative and visual effects agencies.

In addition to my academic, political, and media projects, I also found ways to help people directly. I had worked in the city of Boston with great partners like Hurmon to provide assistance to those who were left behind. I worked with a number of programs for our veterans and their family members (the Boot Campaign, Guard Support of Massachusetts, the Glen Doherty Memorial Foundation, the Michael J. Medders Foundation, and Operation Send-a-Box). I worked with different partners to help convicts—or better put, "returning citizens"—in their postprison lives. Although my wife and I tend to help locally in our community, state, and country, we also believe we should assist beyond our borders. We have partnered with projects in Nigeria and Uganda and with the great organization World Vision in places of need like Mexico and Afghanistan.

The anchoring conviction behind all these partnerships, projects, and aspirations was that each of God's children—each and every one, including you—should be encouraged in their special role and place. The partnership and project efforts may have been ill-constructed, they may have been ill-advised, and certainly many of them were unsuccessful. But they were motivated by the objective that all would know their liberty and their freedom as children of God—and would know that they really *matter.*

Which brings me to 2016 and that wilderness feeling. I won't bog down this book with the degree of disappointment I felt when two unsuitable candidates were nominated for president of the United States, and particularly disappointed in my own political party, the Republican Party. I wasn't alone in that feeling; in a poll taken in September 2016, only 33 percent of Americans were satisfied with the presidential candidates, far and away the lowest percentage in history.[6] The dissatisfaction was experienced across the board, by all types of Americans—young and old, rich and poor, Republican and Democrat, black and white and Latino and Asian. I shared the depth of sadness and despair of the American people in light of these leadership options and felt I had to try to do something to offer hope and alternatives.

I had largely believed my mission was to serve in a supporting role until this point. As I often describe it, I had served as a "stagehand" of sorts, to help the right people occupy the public stage.

Something happened in 2016. I strongly believed that the leadership "on the stage" in the political and faith worlds was letting down the American people. I literally couldn't sleep, and I didn't feel I could live with myself if I didn't step up and try to provide constructive solutions to the problem at hand.

So after spending the first months of 2016 trying to work within the system (I can't tell you how many fiery conversations I had with governors, senators, and other leaders within my party), I quit my political party and founded a national organization called Better for America.

Through BFA, we worked to create ballot access across the country for an important figure to run for president outside the party system. I traipsed around the country along with my colleagues, meeting and interviewing political and financial and media leaders, trying to catalyze a national movement. We spoke with pretty much every one of the national figures you may have heard being discussed who were considering a presidential run in 2016.

When I started BFA, I considered my efforts to be like those of a flag-bearer on an old battlefield (I always thought of the Civil War battlefields when I imagined it). The previous flag-bearers had gone down, the flag (a symbol for leadership and the spirit of this great nation) was on the ground, and I was picking it up. While I knew that the odds of rallying the forces were low, I figured I had to scoop up that tattered and muddied flag anyway and wave it high for a while. Either the troops would rally, or we would be left alone on the battlefield and the mission lost.

After working for the best part of 2016 to address the dissatisfaction felt by so many of my fellow Americans, and spending a lot of money trying, it became clear that my mission had failed. No national figure stepped forward to challenge the Republican and Democratic candidates, and the 2016 election left us a bitterly divided nation. And for the first time, at age fifty, I felt the embarrassment of stepping onto a public stage and failing.

I now had a track record of some interesting life experiences, some successes through my partnerships and projects with many great people, and at least one public embarrassment. With our nation so divided, like so many, I found myself frustrated with our nation's leadership (or lack thereof). As I considered what I might do about it, I wondered whether perhaps I'd put too much energy into trying to get others to do what I myself had never done: run for political office.

As I had never previously thought I should lead, you might imagine that this idea prompted some serious soul-searching. I asked people who had known me for decades: Is running for office consistent with what you know about me, what my abilities are, and who I am? I asked political experts (pollsters and other political insiders who had worked on impor-tant campaigns across the country) for their views and their best analysis of me and the political circumstances. I even asked some great leaders who had themselves run for meaningful national or statewide offices (some who had won and some who had lost). Even more shocking than the first "maybe I should run" thought was that the feedback I received was uniformly positive. Not that they said I would win, of course, merely that I was suitable for the task and that the mission was credible. Given all sorts of factors to consider in the Massachusetts political climate and the ever-evolving political dynamics, certainly no one would have predicted that I would win.* Nevertheless, given the relatively unfavorable ratings of my opponent (if I reached the general election), I had a reasonable shot.

Everyone I consulted with—both in advance of running and throughout my campaign—thought there was a high probability I would win the primary, given patterns from past elections, a pool of relatively unknown candidates, and my clear spending advantages in a small primary (I was the only candidate able to spend meaningfully on advertising).†

My one ironclad principle in this entire process was that I was willing to endure anything—bad press (got lots of that), betrayal (the political world is remarkable in its duplicity, so its bad reputation is deserved), poor public speaking performances on my part (yup, experienced that too), and great financial cost and sacrifice—as long as I won the primary and had a chance to proclaim my "Uniting America" message for the sixty-three days after the primary and before the general election.‡

That was the point of the entire exercise, to preach what I described as a "civic gospel" of uniting America. When I had rolled out my Better for America efforts in 2016, my basic premise was that Americans were generally all right. We just had been presented with poor leadership options, and we needed, and deserved, better. By now my thinking had shifted to some degree. Yes, we needed better leaders; but we also needed to make decisions as citizens to unite together. The most fundamental of

---

* Reminds me of a couple of great lines: "It's tough to make predictions, especially about the future" (attributed to many, although often thought to have been a "Yogiism" from baseball-playing philosopher Yogi Berra) and "Never make predictions—especially about the future" (often attributed to Samuel Goldwyn).

† In sharing this, I am *not* intending to convey this for the accuracy of the viewpoints (obviously turned out the input was inaccurate!) but merely noting that this was the universe of information available to me. My opponents in the campaign are good people with considerable talent and great records of public service (who I am sure had much different inputs on the likelihood of success), and I had tremendous respect for their strengths and this process. Given that, I of course took their candidacies very seriously and hired the best political minds in the country to carefully evaluate their messages, platforms, and resources, and our path to victory.

‡ In a curious feature of Massachusetts politics, the primary is held after Labor Day, only a few short weeks—in this case, nine—prior to the general election.

**A campaign team unlike any other!**

our American problems aren't inherently Democratic or Republican, and the solutions won't be Democratic or Republican; they will be *American* solutions. One thing about my campaign that I am truly and deeply proud of is that it looked and felt like no political campaign ever. We had black, white, Latino, and Asian teammates in campaign management; but perhaps even more striking was that our management team was comprised of Democrats, Independents, Green Party members, and yes, even Republicans (which I ran as). And in that spirit, my wife and I developed—alongside my campaign—a parallel not-for-profit effort unsurprisingly called Uniting America. Uniting America convened non-partisan public conversations spotlighting areas in need and served with those working on the ground to heal America's deepest and most pressing wounds.*

---

\* At Uniting America, we served and worked with partners already advancing compassionate, practical solutions in the following areas and more: mental health, addiction treatment, and the opioid crisis; race and racial reconciliation; veterans empowerment and care; supporting first responders; providing educational and economic opportunities for all; helping address challenges in the adoption and

From time to time I would experience doubts about my initial deliberation process and decision. When I decided to join this race and become a Senate candidate, was I just fooling myself?* I suspect many of you might feel the same way and have similar questions. "Am I kidding myself? Am I cut out for this?" "Do I have what it takes, or am I just embarrassing myself?" And my most important question of the moment: "Will I at least win the primary?" I would circle back with the more important figures in my life inside and outside the campaign (Jean, pollsters, speech coaches who had worked with great politicians, campaign consultants with extensive experience in large-scale campaigns, and spiritual directors in my life). To my surprise, the answer always came back the same: a consensus and unanimous yes that my original conclusions were sound ones and that I should stay the course.

I was in total campaign mode around the clock for eighteen months. I traveled throughout the state for nearly a year, meeting thousands of folks with salt-of-the-earth wisdom who gave me hope about the common decency of people. I loved all that; I loved the opportunity to meet people doing so many interesting things around the state! I had world-class coaches teach me how to deliver a speech and how to do live television interviews, I made commercials (they aren't as easy as they look), and I hit hundreds of town meetings and state fairs and street festivals.

Then it came time to vote. Given the results of my internal polling, as well as the internal polling on our race by others, and the surveying

---

foster care ecosystem; balancing concerns of security and compassion in immigration; addressing the "least of these" in society, including those who are homeless and fall outside the safety net; and taking on human costs of mass incarceration and recidivism.

* This happened a couple of times over the eighteen months, often when I was being asked to spend more money and wondered whether this was a foolish venture. I hesitate to even admit this, but the "more money" I'm referring to was unfortunately in the millions. But each time my wife and I evaluated the next round of unanticipated costs, we would ultimately conclude that when God asks you to proceed down a path (like this campaign), and in your best judgment you believe that it is the right thing to do, he isn't saying "as long as it costs you less than X," whatever X might be. God gave us the money to use, and as I shared earlier, we never expected to have it—and some things are right to do, whatever their cost.

calls we placed to 100,000 expected voters (a big number when you expect only 150,000 in the primary), my team was confident.*

Getting to cast a vote for myself was an unforgettable moment. There was something about the signs, the activity, and the energy of civic involvement that pierced my soul. This was just the first step before being able to face down the incumbent in the general election, but it was still momentous, a big honor to vote for myself in a democratic election. "I've never felt more American," I thought as I went home to write the victory speech I would deliver at the celebratory event I would host when the results were announced.

We'd rented a big room for our supporters to wait out the evening as the votes trickled in. I'd been in many similar election-night rooms before, and I knew that sometimes the evening stretches into the morning. We made sure they had plenty of food and drink, and a great R & B band too.

The core team—the leaders of the campaign plus family—was tucked away in a hotel suite, buckling down for the big night. Then, almost as soon as we'd settled in, we received the news.

I was losing. Badly. As in, losing by nearly thirty percentage points badly, reflected in all the districts and towns that were reporting early. And that meant a thirty-plus percentage point polling error badly. I am a big fan of stats and follow sports and political numbers closely, and I had never seen an outcome this far off. I'd invested eighteen months (and,

---

* As you would probably guess, the polling of "other candidates" didn't include that of the candidates in my race, but rather others who were polling in the race. For those who don't follow these matters as closely as a stats geek like myself, there are two polling worlds: internal polling (which is paid for and conducted by the candidate and campaign) and public polling (which is done by a third party). The objective of internal polling is to be as accurate as possible to guide your campaign's decision making; that said, beware of any internal polling that is shared publicly by a campaign. The campaigns are under no obligation to share the results, and if they are shared, there is a good chance they have been skewed in one way or another to achieve some sort of public objective, sending a message the campaign wants to convey to the electorate. In our campaign, the last public polling done several weeks ahead of the campaign had *not* predicted my victory, but it was only prior to our spending millions in public advertising to our narrow-targeted universe. Our internal polling trends after our advertising spending reflected a favorable result.

painfully, many millions of dollars) in this effort, yet everything unraveled very quickly. The one ironclad "I will go through anything, but I can't and won't go through a primary loss" commitment was now tested.

The hunt began for our immediate family members who had wandered down into the party area so we could let them know before the room found out. Then I had to figure out how to handle the impending concession—when just minutes before I had been practicing my victory speech in the ballroom. The logistics of losing are more daunting than one might think. I would have to call the winner, then go out and deliver an uplifting speech—one I had not prepared—and do this all before my ardent supporters went home dejected.

One by one, family members who had been called into the suite sat down on the couch, not knowing what was going on.

"It's done," Jean told them.

"What do you mean it's done?" they invariably responded. "What's done?"

Already dejected, we had to see my abject failure on all their faces over and over again. They were shocked.

"But we just got here," someone declared.

Yes, that's how badly I lost. It wasn't even close. I not only lost an election, I was humiliated. The magnitude of the errors in analysis and judgment was staggering. Let me get a little "numbers wonky" to show you what I mean. Approximately 150,000 primary voters were projected in most models (yes, the Massachusetts Republican Party numbers are small), and the day after Labor Day was projected to be a slow voting day (would people coming back from summer vacation be paying attention?). Instead, an additional 120,000 voters showed up at the polls—blowing the doors off the estimate, with an 80 percent increase in voter turnout. The theory had been that if more people showed at the polls, the better my chances, because I was the only candidate advertising on television and radio (at least at any scale), and the "extra" voters not as fully plugged in would have seen only my ads. Instead, the exact opposite occurred.

When you lose in the Super Bowl by a field goal, you know you were close and that one decision or play might have made a difference. When you lose by five touchdowns and your opponent gains 500 yards on offense and you gain 150 yards, you were never fully in the game. That is how pronounced the loss was. A good argument could be made that *nothing I could have done over eighteen months of campaigning and spending would have or could have affected the outcome.* When looked at that way, there was never a chance to win the primary, the only thing I "had to" do; yet curiously, given all the regular "taking the best knowledge and inputs" soundings I had done, I didn't second-guess that I was supposed to run.

How do you make sense of that? The sting of the loss and the sense of "What in the world just happened?" didn't dissipate quickly. I spent weeks bouncing between states of disbelief, embarrassment, frustration, and disillusionment. The nights were long, as sleep didn't come easy, and the mornings might have been worse, as I continually woke to the same unchanged reality, like Bill Murray's character in *Groundhog Day.*

There is no guidebook for the steps required after you lose an election—no one warns you about what happens next. One day you are working at high gear with thirty teammates and a statewide alliance, and for the next nine weeks before the general election, every day has been carefully scheduled to put all your chips on the table and explode onto the national stage. For example, we had purchased a large RV to do the classic "put big campaign pictures on side of campaign bus and travel around the state" for the stretch run, and my game plan was to literally run across the state in that short period. (Gimmicky? Sure, that's fair. But while people had walked across states they were running in before, no one had run across a state. And I was excited about the "I am running for you" metaphor!) The morning of September 4, every plan was dead, the RV had to be sold, and each member of the team was on their way to their next role in life.

Seasoned veterans describe losing an election as being like experiencing a death in the family. You experience a great personal sense of loss (as do your teammates as they head their separate ways), while the rest of the world still moves in its own rhythms, with no cognizance of your sense of loss. One of your roles is almost pastoral, as you try to help close teammates in their own grieving processes. As forlorn as I felt, I know on some days some of my teammates felt a whole lot worse.*

Add to this experience the very painful challenges my youngest son was dealing with at the time (as any parent knows, when your children are in pain, nothing feels right), which were far more difficult. While his challenges did keep me from brooding more than I already was, I struggled to find answers for the both of us.

Within five weeks of the primary, I was away with some teammates in our Vermont office, and when out on a run, I inexplicably had a sudden stroke. In the middle of my run, I felt a complete loss of bodily control on one side of my body. What you might not know (I certainly didn't) is that if one half of your body gives out, you start to powerlessly spiral in ever-tighter circles in the direction of the paralyzed half until you hit the ground, because one half of your body is unable to sustain your body's weight. I managed to roll off the country road I was on and onto the grass on the side of the road. Fortunately, the paralysis lasted only a few short minutes, and I was able to slowly force myself to my feet and start to walk home.

After a few minutes I felt a little bit better and thought, "Hey, why not see if I can run the rest of the way? It is getting dark and I have to get home somehow!" My effort seemed to be going well when suddenly the same paralysis took hold of me, and this time *much* more aggressively. The tight spiral-fall to the ground happened even more quickly, and I

---

* And one more thing they don't tell you about and you aren't prepared for: A campaign in many ways is like a business. But unlike a traditional business, if you lose a political campaign, the entire entity comes to an immediate halt, and you have to begin dismantling what you worked so hard to build. For us, it meant we were sending back hundreds of thousands of dollars to people who had contributed to my general election fund (which under election laws you can't use if you don't win the primary). While at the same time vendors are asking you to pay them many hundreds of thousands of dollars you owe them. Super painful! Especially making payments to vendors that had steered you to make bad campaign and spending decisions with bad information, like the car mechanic who asks you to pay them $1,000 when the car they "fixed" is in worse shape than when you brought it in.

ended up in a heap on the double lines in the middle of the road. I knew *this* wasn't good and tried to roll off the road, but it was a much greater challenge this time. A kind passerby stopped his car in the middle of the road to block traffic and came to offer assistance. Not only could I not move, but this time I struggled to form coherent thoughts, and for a few short minutes (which felt like an eternity), I couldn't talk. Although this happened on a very modestly traveled road in the country, after a few minutes a number of neighbors had stopped and joined the effort to assist me. A local veterinarian was summoned to gauge my situation and offer assistance (a veterinarian is close enough, right?), and I gradually regained my functioning.

What did I feel and think at the time? After the first "I hope this isn't serious" feelings subsided, when my capacities returned, I mainly felt embarrassment and a desire not to impose on these good folks. I persuaded them that I was fine, that if one of these kind "first responders" could drive me to our Vermont office, all would be well. Shortly after a kind gentleman dropped me off at the office, the ambulance and paramedics arrived, and I also managed to persuade them that I was just fine and didn't need to go to the hospital.

When my wife, Jean, heard about these developments later in the evening (given I was away, I *might* have kept the details of the story from her—but the Red Sox were playing the Yankees in the American League Division Series, so there was important business to attend to!), she intervened from the Boston area to ensure that the teammates on the trip with me would make me go to the hospital—but only after I watched the Red Sox eliminate the Yankees, so I personally considered that a win of sorts. Yes, even to me all of this—starting to run a second time after the first paralyzed fall, thinking this wasn't serious enough to share with my wife, and refusing to go to the hospital until forced—sounds a little crazy. But I still prefer to think of it as being steadfast and committed!

When they took the tests at the emergency room in the middle of the night, it was determined that I had had a stroke (at *that* point I became grateful I had gone to the hospital, because this now felt serious). I was hospitalized for a few days as they figured out the root cause. There were no immediate answers, but after more tests over the next month, all the experts seemed to agree that my stroke was similar to a "bug" in my body's central operating system and unlikely to recur. Still, as you can probably guess, the event remained unsettling.

One of the projects I didn't mention earlier was our work on a five-hundred-acre farm and retreat center in the Woodstock and Killington, Vermont, area, a beautiful property spread across the rolling green hills overlooking the Ottauquechee River valley. The central farmhouse was built in the early 1800s, and the farm has served as a center of hospitality for many years. In more recent years, the farm had served as a spiritual retreat center for thousands of students from colleges and universities around the Northeast. We have continued to use it in that capacity, as well as a place where leaders and academics and cultural creatives convene and retreat to find inspiration. Bottom line—OQ Farm has been a special space for many people, with a history of hospitality; rolling hills; and alpacas, sheep, and horses.[7]

So what do you do when your health is a little questionable, your family is in pain, and you have lost your sense of direction? I went back to the most basic of activities. I drove to the farm to do some manual labor (despite the objections of some concerned family members, given the stroke). Once there, I put myself under the direction of the farm's manager, a wonderful guy named Rick Chubbuck. I don't have much in the way of farming skills (not even a gentleman's farming skills, as that old saying goes), but I am pretty good at manual labor when I set my mind to it. Rick knew my skills were limited, and he set me to the most basic of tasks—clearing rocks from a field that needed to be tilled and reseeded. There's nothing like working hard in the mud of an open field to clear the mind. Though I experienced a kind of tired different from the sort I was used to, my spirit was energized.

My American Awakening partner Calvin Lee and
me after a good day of work at OQ Farm.

During those days in the field, I thought about all the wonderful people I had met over the preceding three years, from Better for America to Uniting America and the Senate campaign. I thought about the despair I saw across the land and how much I felt for the many Americans experiencing great fear and pain. I thought about my own fear and pain and the experiences and challenges of my life and how we are really all in this together. And the idea of this book emerged from those fields.

I remained highly uncertain about my course, however. The purpose questions emerged, since I had been conclusively shoved off the leadership stage in the election. *Is helping to improve this country really my mission? Is this why I am on this earth at this moment in time? Is spreading a message of purpose and togetherness what the next decade of my life should hold?* Since everything I'd tried in recent years had at least some disappointment attached to it, if not abject failure, why did I think anyone would want to listen?

And so, after an extensive time of wandering in the wilderness of disappointment—hoping that J. R. R. Tolkien's famous "Not all those who wander are lost" line was true—here I am, trying to tell you about purpose.

The search for purpose has gone on for thousands of years; it seems every few years, there's one must-read book that reminds us of the deeper question of purpose and attempts to provide an answer. I have looked behind the corners and underneath the rocks of the various intellectual traditions and found that similar themes are woven throughout.

From my life and experience and study of hundreds of books, essays, articles, speeches, and experiments from the last three thousand years, I've found that the greatest thinkers and traditions are in agreement. They all point to finding yourself and your purpose through living as you were uniquely designed, in a way that is good and true and virtuous. They each point to purpose being grounded, ultimately, in believing in something greater than yourself. Unfortunately, this is not how we understand happiness in our modern age.

You—uniquely you, there can be no other you—are made magnificently and wonderfully, to be and do magnificent and wonderful things. Saint Irenaeus said it this way: "The glory of God is man fully alive."[8] You were created in the image of one from whom all good and beauty and justice and mercy are sourced.[9] That fact cannot be made any smaller or greater, and you can't stop it from being true, even if you want to. You can, of course, forget it, ignore it, and wander away from it—nearly all of us do that for great portions of our lives.

Being created in God's image is not the same as being perfect—there are real challenges and limitations in all of us. But in your genetic code, you are marked as loved and special and unique, and living in that reality is something that can't be taken away.

Hollywood star Chris Pratt spoke to this point when he shared his surprising nine rules of life at the 2018 MTV Video Music Awards. Among uniquely Chris Pratt-ish insights (one rule informs the audience how best to poop if you are using a restroom at a party), he offered his take on purpose. Rule five is "God loves you and God wants the best for you." Rule nine is "Nobody is perfect. People will tell you that you are perfect just the way you are. You are not! You are imperfect. You always will be, but there is a powerful force that designed you that way, and if you are willing to accept that, you will have grace. And grace is a gift. . . . Do not forget that. Don't take that for granted."[10]

If Chris Pratt and his inimitable style isn't your cup of tea, Franciscan friar Richard Rohr offers a more elegant presentation:

> Within us there is an inner, natural dignity. (You often see it in older folks.)
>
> An inherent worthiness that already knows and enjoys. (You see it in children.)
>
> It is an immortal diamond waiting to be mined and it is never discovered undesired.
>
> It is a reverence humming within you that must be honored.
>
> Call it the soul, the unconscious, deep consciousness, or the indwelling Holy Spirit.
>
> Call it nothing.
>
> It does not need the right name or right religion to show itself.
>
> It does not even need to be understood. It is usually wordless.
>
> It just is, and shows itself best when we are silent, or in love, or both.
>
> I will call it the True Self here.
>
> It is God-in-All-Things yet not circumscribed by any one thing.[11]

As Pratt and Rohr describe, this dimension of you is so much a part of you that it can't be stripped away or even ultimately changed. We are instruments of an inner, natural dignity, an inherent worthiness, a reverence inside us all that wants to be honored. And as we will explore in later chapters, each one of us also has our own unique contribution to the whole of humanity.

When you see your life through this prism, you get a sense that God was aware of us long before we were aware of him. In *The Purpose Driven*

*Life*, Rick Warren wrote, "Your life is not a result of random chance, fate, or luck. . . . Everything that happens to you has spiritual significance. Everything. . . . His purpose for your life predates your conception. He [God] planned it before you existed."[12]

Remarkably, that love and design and purpose are in play even if we aren't aware of them. This is all oddly liberating. Who we are and what we do are bigger than any one of us, and we are merely trying to find the clues as to how we can participate in our own purpose.

This may seem too "faith-filled" for your tastes, and I understand that may not work for some. But as Nobel laureate—and atheist—Bertrand Russell acutely observed, "Unless you assume a God, the question of life's purpose is meaningless."[13] Rick Warren agrees. "You were made *by* God and *for* God—and until you understand that, life will never make sense," he wrote. "It is only in God that we discover our origin, our identity, our meaning, our purpose, our significance, and our destiny. Every other path leads to a dead end."[14]

These are sobering words, especially for those of us who feel we've already come to some dead ends.

One of the greatest American contributions to the world of spirituality was the creation of Alcoholics Anonymous in the 1930s. Bill Wilson and his founding partners came out of a Judeo-Christian understanding of the world, but they didn't expressly hardwire a Christian worldview into the program. Instead, knowing that people who needed to find their footing and purpose had to start somewhere, they instructed program participants who were searching for health to "believe that a Power greater than ourselves could restore us to sanity."[15] This was often described as finding the higher power of one's understanding, with the clear implication that everyone didn't have to agree on a definition of God. That was followed by a "decision to turn our will and our lives over to the care of God as we understood him."[16]

You have to believe in something bigger than yourself to find where you stand and why—until you find that, you are not only wandering, you may also be lost.

The latest scientific findings generally support these purpose principles and indicate that purpose is correlated with all sorts of positive life and health outcomes.

First, people with a greater sense of purpose live longer. A *Lancet* study showed that people over age sixty-five who ranked higher on eudaemonic well-being were less likely to die in the next eight and a half years.* Among the people who had scored in the lowest quartile on that measure of well-being, 29 percent died, while over the same time period, of those who had scored in the highest quartile, only 9 percent died.[17] Another study found that "having a purpose in life appears to widely buffer against mortality risk across the adult years."[18]

People with a greater sense of purpose also score higher on tests of memory and executive functioning according to a study of more than three thousand adults in Canada and the United States.[19]

People who have a sense of purpose also live healthier lives. We are all probably aware that the immune system influences whether we get sick or not, but it also plays a critical role in many measures of health and indeed can trigger feelings of depression, loneliness,[20] and cardiovascular disease.[21] Those who strongly believe "I have something to contribute to society," or "My life has a sense of direction," exhibit highly favorable immune system activity. Conversely, those who report they don't sense a larger purpose or don't make contributions to the lives of others (but say they are happy) exhibit immune system activity that tends to result in poor health.[22] In other words, pursuing our own self-care without a larger purpose or investment in others may actually be detrimental to our health.

Further, a focus on happiness and pleasure† is associated with higher

---

\*    Recall from our earlier discussion on Aristotle that eudaemonia involves the good performance of one's function.

†    These are the seven items defining the scale: (1) How happy I am at any given moment says a lot about how worthwhile my life is. (2) If I don't feel happy, maybe there is something wrong with me. (3) I value things in life only to the extent that they influence my personal happiness. (4) I would like

levels of loneliness and depression.[23] Those who believe "How happy I am says a lot about how worthwhile my life is," or "If I don't feel happy, maybe there is something wrong with me," reported the highest levels of loneliness and depression.

And consider one more item: studies show that those who pray or meditate frequently are 47 percent more likely to have a sense of mission and purpose.[24]

So science tells us that people with a sense of purpose live longer, are healthier, think more clearly and quickly, and are less lonely and depressed. And if you actively commit yourself to something greater than yourself, you are much more likely to have a sense of purpose.

———

Though our family mission statement hung on that bulletin board for years, I hadn't read it in some time. But after a small house fire—yes, right in the middle of the campaign—forced us to rebuild sections of our home, I took the paper down and read it again.

My 1998 self reminded my 2018 self of who I am and what I was made to be: that I am to help people find their special role and place on the planet, that I should be "unafraid to fail," and that I should "never give in—never, ever, ever," echoing Winston Churchill's great reminder in World War II. We *can't* give in, no matter what we face.

It may sound mystical for me to say my 1998 drafting of our mission prepared me for my Better for America and Senate losses. A sense of purpose helps mitigate the devastating effects of failure because our achievements or failures don't define us. If anything, these failures refine us into the people we were created to be.

We're each on a lifelong journey to *be* who we were created to be, the best we can, today, that is, living our purpose daily. And also to be

---

to be happier than I generally am. (5) Feeling happy is extremely important to me. (6) I am concerned about my happiness even when I feel happy. (7) To have a meaningful life, I need to feel happy most of the time.

refined by our successes and failures, triumphs and tragedies, and *become* the truest versions of ourselves so we can make our maximum contribution to the world.

When we're being who we were created to be and becoming the truest versions of ourselves, as we wander, we are never actually lost, however much it may occasionally feel we are. And no matter who we are and where we find ourselves, we can never give in. Never, ever, ever.

# The Kingston Family Mission Statement

Our Mission is to live every day and every experience passionately and fully in a fashion pleasing to our Heavenly Father.

We believe that our Father loves his children completely and without condition, and has a special role and place for each child.

In our home we will show each of God's children—both inside our family and out—that love, and encourage each to find his or her special role and place.

To that end, we will:

- accept God's grace, love and acceptance;
- see the beauty of God's hand everywhere;
- be grateful in all things;
- excel in our service of the perfect Master;
- play hard and have fun!;
- love our friends and our enemies;
- recall that the "first shall be last, and the last shall be first"—and see station and status clearly;
- serve when we find need;
- meet injustice with fairness;
- fire our passions;
- moderate our excesses;
- refuse to accept unfounded propositions, and instead seek truth;
- be inspired by the uniqueness and variety of God's children;
- forgive freely;
- judge no person, as each is subject to God's grace;
- be unafraid to fail;
- never give in—never, ever, ever.

Knowing the triumph and transcendence of God's love, we live boldly each day, seeing in the challenges of that day the promise of the Kingdom to come.

# CHAPTER 3

# YOU LONG FOR RENEWAL

## FIND MORE IN LESS

One Saturday in 2000, professors Sheena Iyengar from Columbia University and Mark Lepper from Stanford University set up a tasting booth at Draeger's Market, an upscale grocery store in Menlo Park, California. The two chose Draeger's because the store offered an extraordinary selection of products—for example, two hundred fifty varieties of mustard, seventy-five varieties of olive oil, and over three hundred varieties of jam. In the tasting booth, Iyengar and Lepper offered shoppers samples of twenty-four jams made by Wilkin & Sons, a company distinguished by the fact that it provides jam to the Queen of England. For sampling a jam, customers received a coupon for one dollar off any jam purchase.

The following Saturday, Iyengar and Lepper once again set up shop in Draeger's Market, providing the same one dollar off any jam purchase to sampling customers. However, this time they reduced the number of jams available to sample. Instead of offering twenty-four varieties to sample, they offered only six.

In their now-famous "jam experiment," Iyengar and Lepper sought to determine the validity of the common belief that the more choices we have, the better off we are. "From classic economic theories of free enterprise," they explained, "to mundane marketing practices that provide customers with entire aisles devoted to potato chips or soft drinks, to important life decisions in which people contemplate alternative career options or multiple investment opportunities, this belief pervades our institutions, norms, and customs. Ice cream parlors compete to offer the most flavors; major fast-food chains urge us to 'Have it our way.'"[1]

By increasing and then limiting customers' jam choices, the two researchers wanted to know which condition would be more effective in compelling customers to buy a jam.

Can you guess what happened?

Of the 242 customers who passed the twenty-four-jam booth, 145, or 60 percent, stopped at the booth to sample jam. In comparison, of the 260 customers who passed the six-jam booth, only 104, or 40 percent, stopped at the booth. Probably no surprise there—more people were attracted to the booth with more choices. But the goal was not to test how many people would stop by the booth but rather how many would choose to *buy* jam because of a greater or lesser number of options. This is where the experiment became interesting.

The results showed that the attractiveness of the twenty-four-jam booth did not translate to jam sales. In fact, the opposite occurred. While nearly 30 percent of the consumers in the six-jar booth subsequently purchased a jar of jam, less than 3 percent of the consumers in the twenty-four-jam booth did so.[2]

In other words, customers presented with a limited number of choices were nearly ten times more likely to purchase a jar of jam than those who were presented with a much wider array of jams to choose from. While one can see the possible limitations of such a simple initial field experiment,* the results led to dozens of follow-up studies. The results of this extensive research are now widely accepted in the social science community and point to the following conclusion: while more options might seem more optimal and liberating, it appears we are more satisfied with fewer choices.

---

* For instance, maybe customers who visited the six-jam booth thought there was something special about the limited offerings, or perhaps the six-jam display was more appealing to more serious jam buyers.

In his viral TED Talk about the paradox of choice, renowned psychologist and author Barry Schwartz shows a cartoon of a parent and child fish in a fishbowl, and the parent fish is telling its offspring, "You can be anything you want to be—no limits."[3] The absurdity of the parent fish's statement is clear. Of course the child fish can't be anything it wants to be; it's in a fishbowl!

Schwartz asks his audience to consider the obvious questions raised by the fishbowl scenario. To free up that child fish to be *truly* all it wants to be, is the parent supposed to liberate it from the fishbowl? Does the parent simply shatter the glass enclosure? Sure, in that case the little fish would no longer have constraints; but it would have some far more serious problems. "The truth of the matter is," explains Schwartz, "if you shatter the fishbowl so that everything is possible, you don't have freedom. . . . You increase paralysis, and you decrease satisfaction. Everybody needs a fishbowl. . . . The absence of some metaphorical fishbowl is a recipe for misery and, I suspect, disaster."[4]

In America, freedom of choice is woven into the fabric of our identity. Perhaps this is no more apparent than in the thousands of choices available to us each day—in the supermarket, at the mall, on the internet, or on social media. And the number of options seems to be only growing. But does the seemingly ever-increasing number of choices do us more harm than good?

"Choice *is* good for us," explains Schwartz, "but its relationship to satisfaction appears to be more complicated than we had assumed. . . . There is diminishing utility in having alternatives; each new option subtracts a little from the feeling of well-being. . . . More [choice] requires increased time and effort and can lead to anxiety, regret, excessively high expectations, and self-blame if the choices don't work out."[5]

Schwartz summarizes the general belief of Western societies: "The more choices people have, the more freedom they have, and the more freedom they have, the more welfare they have."[6] He describes a supermarket near his home that—like Draeger's Market in the jam experiment—offers 175 salad dressings.

Even something as foundational as our identity includes choices today, Schwartz points out. "We don't inherit an identity; we get to invent it. . . . So everywhere we look, big things and small things, material things and lifestyle things, life is a matter of choice. And the question is: Is this good news or bad news? And the answer is 'yes.'"[7]

The surprising effect, as Schwartz and others have indicated, is that even if we manage to make choices in the midst of exponential options, we are more stressed while doing so and likely to end up less satisfied with our decisions. This is because the more options that are available to us, the easier it is to be disappointed. Why? We really want to make the right or optimized choice for ourselves, but if there are more choices, you'll never be able to examine every possible option before making a decision—and therefore we are afraid we didn't pick that *perfect* one. One common shorthand for this problem in the modern world is FOBO, or "fear of better options."

If you've been reading this and feel a bit of resistance rising up (What do you mean, more choice isn't better?), you aren't alone. Most of us have lived our lives believing more choices equals more freedom and more freedom equals a better well-being. This is America, after all!

But maybe if we consider our choices and freedom from a different vantage point, we can see more clearly what studies like the jam experiment are revealing not just *to* us but also *about* us.

## More Money, More Happiness?

In 2019 Tony Bennett and the University of Virginia men's basketball team won their first NCAA Championship title in program history. After the season—Bennett's tenth with the Cavaliers (also known as Wahoos, as serious fans know)—UVA president Jim Ryan offered Bennett a substantial raise. As "it is time for a raise" circumstances go, this was a pretty good one. Bennett had built an outstanding record in his decade at UVA, his program had been scandal-free (hard to do these days in the NCAA), and of course, he had just won a national championship. And what's more, this scenario is often one in which the most successful coaches are enticed away by fancier programs, NBA teams, and substantial compensation packages elsewhere. And on one level, why not? Looking for the next challenge, for greater prestige, or to make more money is part of human nature, and at times even human greatness.

Bennett declined the raise, making national news in the process.

He not only declined the raise but also asked the university to focus instead on additional compensation for his staff and improvements that would benefit the program. The final exclamation point was a $500,000 pledge from Tony and his wife, Laurel, toward a career-development program launched for current and former UVA men's basketball players.[8]

Bennett explained his decision: "I have more than enough," and added, "As the saying goes: Don't mess with happiness. Certainly there have been other opportunities, but I love the college game, I love what this university stands for. . . . I love being here and continuing to try to build."[9]

Bennett said no to the raise largely because he understood that his happiness isn't tied to his compensation or his bank account but instead to his purpose—his role in the growth and success of the young men, the basketball program, and the university he cares so deeply for.

As we discovered together earlier in the chapter, more choices and more freedom can often result in less happiness. Could Tony Bennett be right that having more money and "stuff"* does not create happiness and in some cases may take away from the happiness you have?

Let's start with a simple principle. We all need some stuff—food and clothes and shelter—to live. But as has been stated throughout the ages, in all religions and philosophies, the degree to which you are attached to money and stuff can either bind you or liberate you. Your attachment, or lack thereof, to money is therefore a very important matter in your approach to life.

---

* For simplicity, I will use *stuff* throughout this section because it cuts across all categories of money, materials, goods, and services.

As we will see, all the data today show that no matter how much money Americans have, we want more.

Take for example the spending of the federal government. Federal government spending is nothing other than the sum of the desires of all the people in the democratic process to "get stuff" (paid for by the government) versus their willingness to pay for stuff (to contribute in taxes). In 2019, in the middle of one of the longest periods of economic growth in history and amid more financial prosperity than we have ever had, we had a $1 trillion deficit in spending by the federal government.[10] Yes, $1 trillion! We received nearly 30 percent more stuff than the amount we were willing to pay for, or $3,000 in extra spending for every American. The only other time we have outspent our means in a period of growth was seventy-five years ago, in the heart of World War II. And at that point, we were outspending our means to keep the world free from Nazism and Japanese imperialism, which was a pretty compelling reason to do so.

However important federal spending may be as a policy matter (and it is), my objective is not to discuss the degree to which taxes for our country should go up or spending should go down. But no matter how you look at it, the "desire to get stuff" ultimately has to meet the "desire to pay for stuff."* This idea is just math and one of the laws of financial gravity (spending ultimately has to be equal to or less than the amount you have available to spend).

We see the same financial problems in our own spending. A recent Pew Charitable Trust study found that 46 percent of Americans spend more than they make every month. Nearly half.[11] And although information concerning the ratio of debt to income for individuals is a little hard to come by, there is a lot of evidence that it has generally been on the rise over the last couple of decades, and after a brief step back during

---

\* Sadly, few seem to appreciate that this imbalance has now created a $24 trillion debt in aggregate, or $72,000 for every man, woman, and child. As a consequence, unless a dramatic turnaround is put into effect, this debt will have to be paid by our children and grandchildren—we consume extra today; they pay for us tomorrow.

the global financial crisis, has advanced meaningfully once again. If that financial/economics talk makes your eyes glaze over, a simple way of saying it is that it seems we want more than we have the capacity to buy at almost every level.*

This imbalance in spending, like any imbalance in life, ultimately catches up with you. If you eat too much food and don't exercise enough, eventually you will carry more weight than you would like. Too much spending, and you will have debt. Debt takes away freedom, and debt adds burden.

- In a 2018 American Psychological Association study, 72 percent of Americans said they felt stressed about money, and 22 percent said they felt "extreme" stress over their finances.[12]
- A 2016 Federal Reserve Bank of Atlanta report linked debt to higher death rates; being seriously delinquent on a debt increased mortality risk 5 percent in the first three months after the bill became delinquent, and a one-hundred-point increase in a person's credit score led to a 4.38 percent decline in mortality risk.[13]
- People who struggle with debt are more than twice as likely to suffer from depression, according to a study by the University of Nottingham in England.[14]

Finally—to no surprise of anyone who has ever been in a meaningful relationship—psychologists observe the strong negative effect of debt (particularly avoidable debt) on relationships.

* One survey (commissioned by Ladder and conducted by OnePoll) looked at Americans' spending on "essential" versus "nonessential" items and found that Americans may be able to afford essentials more easily than they think, just by tweaking their spending habits. The average American spends $1,497 per month on nonessential items, according to new research. That can add up to almost $18,000 a year—more than a million dollars over the course of an adult lifetime. Despite spending $1,497 per month on nonessential items, 58 percent of Americans feel there are important things they can't afford.

While Jesus certainly made a number of well-known statements, some of the most renowned were part of his Sermon on the Mount. In that "speech," Jesus offered liberation from an undue attachment to money and stuff.

> "Therefore I tell you, do not be anxious about your life, what you will eat or what you will drink, nor about your body, what you will put on. Is not life more than food, and the body more than clothing? Look at the birds of the air: they neither sow nor reap nor gather into barns, yet your heavenly Father feeds them. Are you not of more value than they? ... And why are you anxious about clothing? Consider the lilies of the field, how they grow: they neither toil nor spin, yet I tell you, even Solomon in all his glory was not arrayed like one of these. But if God so clothes the grass of the field, which today is alive and tomorrow is thrown into the oven, will he not much more clothe you?"[15]

Jesus mentions Solomon, an ancient king who famously had more stuff than anyone *ever*, and provides a stark illustration of the "more money, not necessarily more happiness" phenomenon. In Solomon's writings in Ecclesiastes, dozens of times he describes how meaningless everything is—indeed, so deep is the sense of unhappiness he describes that it makes for a painful read. He summed up the feeling this way: "So I hated life, because the work that is done under the sun was grievous to me. All of it is meaningless, a chasing after the wind. I hated all the things I had toiled for under the sun, because I must leave them to the one who comes after me."[16]

That is quite a statement from one of the wealthiest people of his day. Although there are few wealthy people willing to speak so directly today, there is widespread evidence that wealth creates no greater happiness in the modern world.

One person who seems to get this is, of all people, six-time Super Bowl champion quarterback Tom Brady. I was deeply struck many years ago by a 2005 *60 Minutes* interview, when Brady confessed, "Why do

I have 3 Super Bowl rings and still think there's something greater out there for me? Maybe a lot of people would say, 'Hey man, this is what it is, I've reached my goal, my dream, my life.' Me, I think, *God, there's gotta be more than this.*"[17]

Brady's dissatisfaction amid his success is similarly exhibited in today's National Basketball Association, where the average salary is $7.5 million dollars. Many dozens of the highest-paid players earn well over $30 million annually, hundreds of millions over the course of their playing careers, and then many more tens or hundreds of millions of dollars in endorsements. You would think that the fame, glamor, huge social media followings, and big money would help in the happiness category, wouldn't you? Yet sadly, that doesn't appear to be the case; during the 2019 MIT Sloan Sports Analytics Conference, NBA commissioner Adam Silver shared that despite the designer clothes and fancy cars, many players in the league feel isolated and unhappy.[18]

Of course, as we discussed in the last chapter, whether or not you are a star point guard like Steph Curry or Ben Simmons, some critical factors determine your happiness. And therefore it stands to reason (and the evidence shows) that if you're feeling unhappy, the number of zeros on your paycheck won't help.

A broader study on the relationship between money and happiness was recently undertaken by a group of University of California economists. In 2008 the *Sacramento Bee* created a database allowing the public to search (by name and department) the precise salary information for the more than three hundred thousand employees who work for California.[19] Having all your salary information on the web, and that of your coworkers too, is a little daunting, right? Researchers sent two groups of people a survey that included questions like "How satisfied are you with your job?" and "How satisfied are you with your wage/salary on this job?" One group had access to the salary database, and one did not.

The economists found that access to the database had a "negative effect on workers paid below the median for their unit and occupation"[20]—so people were *unhappy* if they found out they made less than others. Was the flip side—that people would be happier if they made more than others—also true? It turns out that it had no effect—making more money did not produce a more satisfying work experience or greater happiness in life.

## Green Pastures and Quiet Waters

I had a revelation when we got the first of our now-three Labradoodles.* Pet ownership and dog oversight are among the many subject matters I know little about. So in my ignorance, I was surprised when Jean purchased a crate for each of them, which I insisted on describing as "cages."

"How can we put them in a cage?" I would ask. "They want their freedom!"

Jean patiently informed me that the dogs longed for the forced constraint of being in their own enclosed spot. In that crate, they would accept their limitations. For example, they would no longer act with their otherwise natural "we are tough guard dogs" instincts, however comical it is for these sweet, furry, domesticated creatures to imagine themselves like Jack London's fierce White Fang. They of course wanted to roam and run but were released to relax and rest by the constraint of the crate.

In a similar vein, around 1000 BC, Israel's King David composed his most famous work—Psalm 23. Many of us know how it begins: "The LORD is my shepherd."[21] I've read or recited that psalm hundreds of times over the years, but I recently noticed something I hadn't observed before.

Why did David say, "He *makes* me lie down in green pastures, he *leads* me beside quiet waters"[22] (emphasis added)? Why must the shepherd—David's reference to God—"Make" and "lead" him to do things that seem obviously desirable, even idyllic? Did David not want peace, beauty, rest?

While scholars of ancient Hebrew history aren't certain what was

---

★    As pet owners everywhere will appreciate, our dogs—Winston, Ranger (another name for Aragorn in the Lord of the Rings), and Lincoln, all named for inspiring leaders—are now so much a part of our lives that we can't remember the days we didn't have them.

happening in King David's life at the time he wrote this psalm, what is known about his life in general is that he had enemies near and far, and some of them were even in his own family, as was the case with his son Absalom, who started a civil war against his father. We also know that as a result of these many enemies, David was frequently on the run, either chasing off an enemy or running from one. While there are certainly accounts of David enjoying the benefits of being a king, his life was busy and burdened. In numerous other psalms, he admits to being exhausted and demoralized. In one instance, he feels utterly hopeless and abandoned, even by God.[23]

While we aren't ancient Israeli kings constantly fending off giant and regular-size adversaries, I believe we can relate to King David's demanding life and perhaps even his feelings of exhaustion and demoralization. Most of all, sometimes life is so demanding and full of so many choices and so much stuff we think we need that we can relate to the reality of needing someone to *make* us lie down in green pastures and *lead* us beside quiet waters.

## More Vacation?

Still, we're not very good at finding those green pastures and quiet waters on a regular basis. While COVID-19 forced us all to shift our working rhythms, we are statistically the most overworked nation on the planet.

- At least 134 countries have laws setting the maximum length of the workweek; the US does not.[24]
- In the US, 85.8 percent of males and 66.5 percent of females work more than forty hours per week.[25]
- According to the International Labor Organization, "Americans work 137 more hours per year than Japanese workers, 260 more hours per year than British workers, and 499 more hours per year than French workers."[26]

I am proud of the American work ethic and believe our approach to work is a wonderful attribute, but dare I ask whether we take it just a bit too far?

According to the U.S. Travel Association, American workers accumulated 705 million unused vacation days in 2017, which amounted to 52 percent of American employees not taking vacation at all that year.[27] Maybe we just need more of the great American pastime we call the family vacation?

On vacation, if you so choose, your life can slow down at least temporarily. (All bets are off if you choose the Disney World option with lots of family!) We perhaps feel for a week or two the way we'd like to feel all the time. Depending on how young the children are or how otherwise crazy your family circumstances, life might feel simpler, and choices may be nicely limited. We soak up the feeling for every last minute until we have to return home. But often we return from vacation to find that the raging flow of life has only increased while we've been out of the current. And then we're playing catch-up. At times it can feel that vacation just isn't worth it.

Obviously, vacations aren't a waste of our time. I'm a big fan of vacations, as I'm sure you are too. But if what we really want is green pastures and quiet waters, then we're going to need something more than a vacation, especially if half of us who work for a living aren't even taking one every year. And, likely, half the vacations we do take end up being more chaotic and stressful than the work we left behind.

## Back to Real Life and the Three Rs

So we returned from vacation (if we were fortunate enough to take one at all), and now we feel behind in the life we came back to. We're buried in overscheduled calendars and an overconsuming lifestyle. Why do we seem so unable to create lives that reflect the rest, beauty, and simplicity we desire? Why can't we orchestrate simpler, slower, green-pastured, quiet-watered lives?

We could just conclude that we're busy, too busy. Life's just busy. The end. That would be the easy answer, but it doesn't help us solve our problem—this inherent urge to chase after something more while feeling an increasing longing for something less. Maybe we can say it this way: the pace of life is faster than our capacity to take in life. The demands of our jobs, relationships, financial obligations, and more keep life moving like a rushing mountain river in springtime. Often we're doing all we can just to keep our heads above water. How do we move at a speed we are comfortable maintaining, without losing touch with the realities of life? We can't just turn the river off. And we don't want to drown.

The solution comes into focus when we consider the purpose vacation is meant to serve in the first place. Let's call them the *R* words, and let's consider the first one that we've already touched on: *rest*.

For thousands of years, the most prominent religions have implored us to rest.

Allowing both body and mind to unwind is the first step in the daily Buddhist practice of meditation, which allows one to remain in sync with the universe.

One of the core tenets of Taoism is a balance of action (being productive) and nonaction (resting, waiting) to avoid bending the universe to your own will. In the Tao Te Ching, Lao Tzu writes:

> Better to stop short than fill to the brim.
> Oversharpen the blade, and the edge will soon blunt.
> Amass a store of gold and jade, and no one can protect it.
> Claim wealth and titles, and disaster will follow.
> Retire when the work is done.
> Such is Heaven's Tao.[28]

The Qur'an references sleep and rest numerous times, using five words to describe the sort of rest a Muslim must seek: *sinah*, which refers to dozing off for a short period due to exhaustion; *nu'ass*, which refers to taking a short nap to reduce stress and fear; *ruqood*, which refers to a long period of sleep; *hojoo*, which refers to normal nighttime sleep; and *subaat*, which refers to disconnecting from one's environment for a period of time.[29]

In the Jewish Torah and the Christian Bible, Genesis 2 explains that on the seventh day of creation, God rested. The Hebrew word used in the Torah is *menuchah*, which translates, simply, "to rest." From this passage the Jewish tradition of Shabbat, or Sabbath, was born.[30]

How much rest do we get in our normal day-to-day? Much less than we used to, according to Gallup, whose recent poll found that Americans average about six hours of sleep a night these days, compared with nine hours a night in 1910.[31] *Forbes* contributor Neil Howe pointed out that technologies like the lightbulb and the internet, which allow us to work 24/7, have propelled our diminishing rest.[32]

There is another *R* word we associate with vacation and that is part of many great moments in life—*recreation*. Although the general use of the word can mean anything from tossing a Frisbee to playing cornhole to Sea-Dooing on the lake, and there is nothing wrong with that, our broad application of it has buried its deeper significance.

The original Latin word is *recreāre* (I know, I told you I wouldn't use too many Latin or Greek words—maybe you will allow me one per chapter!), which generally translates as "create again" or "renew." The first English use of the word was in reference to refreshing or curing a sick person. Recreation is fundamentally about re-creating ourselves through activity.

During the best vacations my family has taken over the years, re-creation definitely happened, even when we weren't aware of it. Our standard family approach is to go someplace (often a place we visit regularly, so there is built-in comfort and established memories) and then do precious little adventurous activity while there. Working out together is usually a big part of our time away. Activities usually include running and hiking as well as low-key athletic games that allow for family participation. Even in recent years, as we have gotten older, we have great family experiences of playing soccer "World Cups," breaking down into two-person teams, as well as competing in a form of soccer "tennis" played on a volleyball court.

During vacation, meals together—which have become way too

infrequent during the normal flow of life, I'm afraid!—have always been an important emphasis. As people throughout the ages have recognized, there is a special magic to breaking bread together. We have countless memories of a nearly ritualized eating experience from our vacations, such as, "We always did that for breakfast there. Remember how great that was?"

Recreation, when done well, scratches that itch we have for a less complicated, more meaningful life, but in an almost teasing sort of way. It makes less become more, but only for a spell. We get a taste of less and we love it. Then more takes over again, and we're back where we started, longing for less.

What we ultimately need, I believe, is the third *R* word—*renewal.* While rest is a temporary break in the action—an eddy in the rushing river of life—and recreation is an act of temporarily re-creating ourselves and our circumstances, renewal is finding the best form of ourselves, the people we are designed to be.

It is easy to fall into anxiety, hopelessness, sadness, and even anger when you consider the state of our country. We are in desperate need of more than rest and recreation. We need renewal. We need to strip away the superficial, extraneous, and meaningless to restore our most meaningful lives. In case we forget what renewal looks like, it is everywhere in the natural world around us.

Every year winter comes, and trees are stripped of their leaves and the grass turns brown. Then spring comes. The world is born again. It's renewed. This is, I believe, a reminder that the work of renewal remains a powerful force—perhaps the *most* powerful force—in the world. But let's not lose sight of the trees for the forest.

Renewal occurs one blade of grass at a time. When only one blade of grass in an acres-wide field turns from brown to green, it's barely noticeable. When every blade of grass turns green again, a field comes to life and serves its purpose. It provides food and shelter and rest and recreation. Each one of us is like a blade of grass. We have the opportunity to participate in the renewal of these American fields by working toward renewing ourselves. We just have to do our part and, if we can, help others do theirs. This is part of my journey toward purpose now, and it could be part of yours.

As we look around this great country, sometimes the fields look barren. Perhaps it's because many of us feel barren ourselves. Maybe our lives are full, but not full of much life. Maybe we are busy but burdened. Successful but unsatisfied. We are brown blades of grass in need of renewal, one blade at a time.

When we feel barren, we sometimes get into an endless cycle of retreat, feeling that we need to take a month off, take a year off, just quit our jobs, move somewhere slower, and start again. What starts with "I just need a vacation" evolves into "I need to get off this hamster wheel." The truth is that we just need to usher restoration into our lives on a regular basis. No more a little rest here, a little recreation there, and a dose of relief in between. If enough of us pursue renewal, the fields of our individual lives, and the fields of this country, will turn to spring again.

A recent family experience provided us with an illustration of this renewal principle. As a consequence of our financial success, for the most part our children have been raised in great comfort, as well as privilege and opportunity. All our children have nevertheless had their meaningful challenges (everyone does!), but one of our sons experienced difficulties he struggled to shake. He had been a terrific athlete and wonderful student, but given a combination of factors, he had lost his motivation and initiative as he advanced through ninth and tenth grades. Some factors were clearly outside his control (a series of very difficult knee injuries requiring reconstruction), while some were within his control. But whatever we tried, we couldn't help him escape a cycle of depression, excess gaming, regular marijuana use, and confrontational household relationships.

After several years of trying different approaches, my wife, Jean, and I had run out of possible solutions to address the situation. We decided that the best available course for our son was something called "wilderness therapy." If you aren't familiar with the concept, the wilderness therapy movement is a relatively modern one, typically designed for adolescents who are stuck in challenging behavioral patterns. Our son was dropped off in the Utah desert with a group of eight to ten young men (the number varied as boys came in and out of the program) with literally no private possessions. No technology, no watches, no jewelry, and no personal clothes (they were provided a desert uniform). This program was a nomadic one—the group did not return to a home base at any point in the program but rather were out in the wilderness with their backpacks, hiking from point to point. Provisions were brought to them, and the counselors rotated in and out week to week, but the boys stayed in the wilderness for as long as their program required.

The boys were stripped down to the most basic of essentials. They did not have chairs to sit on in the desert until they earned them (a reward that took many weeks to earn). They slept under the stars on that dusty, hard ground every night (occasionally moving under tarps strung from trees if bad weather rolled in). They didn't shower (only periodically washing out of a large water pail), which had the effect you might expect on the hygiene of adolescent boys. And they learned to manage their own food rations, to prepare food themselves, and, in an important rite of passage, to start their own fires with the most primitive of elements, something that became an important point of pride as they developed the skill and passed it along to newbies in the group.

Their movements were monitored (they had to request permission to be out of sight lines, and when they were, they had to call out their names every five seconds to establish contact), and their shoes were taken away at night to ensure everyone stayed in camp. At certain key points, they were allowed to be off by themselves for thirty-six to forty-eight-hour periods to further dial up their self-reliance.

Quite a picture, isn't it?

Stripped down to the most basic of elements and relearning how to live, the boys found purpose and meaning. Their bonds with one another and support for one another became extremely strong. In our visits there, we saw that togetherness and community and common cause yielded a demonstrable peace in their spirits. We sensed that our son was more himself when he was out there than he had been in many years, and since his return home, he has consistently applied the lessons he learned in the wilderness. In our conversations with counselors far and wide, we have heard that 95 percent of young men have the same "wow, I am glad I did that" experience.

What happened? The young men traded all the comforts of home (food, shelter, bingeing Netflix, and playing video games) for almost nothing in the wilderness, but with purpose of mind and heart amid strong community, they found something far exceeding normal pleasures and comforts. Seeing their experience, I have often thought it would be good to have more easily accessible adult wilderness experiences—couldn't this help some of us bring life back to our own blades of brown grass?

## Back to the Beginning

If we want to seek renewal, where do we begin? Let me leave you with a suggestion that has worked for me and for many throughout the ages. The Jewish Sabbath is a tradition that was instituted when Moses famously returned from Mount Sinai and gave the Israelites the Ten Commandments. The tenth commandment is "Remember the Sabbath day by keeping it holy."[33] The point of the day was, and still is, renewal. You, like the God of the Jewish tradition, can give yourself the seventh day to rest. Give your body, mind, and spirit a breather. Be with those you love. Enjoy the day. Set aside your wallet and any compulsion to shop and spend. Instead, take in the beauty around you. Take a nap. Take a long walk. Be restored. In this way, the day is made holy because we allow ourselves to remember the simple things in life that God provides—good food, lingering laughter, loved ones, and space to lounge. The shade of a tree and the sound of a trickling stream are satisfying enough.

I was a mess. It was my first semester at Harvard Law School. I was the last person accepted into my 1994 class, accepted off the waiting list just days before the semester started. I had to move the next day from Philadelphia, Pennsylvania, to Cambridge, Massachusetts. I was completely unprepared for the adventure to come, joining very intelligent classmates from around the world who had been preparing for this journey for many months. And I was scheduled to get married in December, just three months away—at the end of the semester but before finals.*

This may no longer be the case, but back in the early 1990s, the first year of law school had a reputation of being an intense proving ground for anxious young students who wanted to make their way in the world, as portrayed in the television series *The Paper Chase* and Scott Turow's bestselling nonfiction book *One L.* I found that the experience lived up to that reputation. As I tried to succeed among my hypermotivated, intense, and supersmart classmates, my approach could best be described by the old folksy phrase "chicken with its head cut off." I scrambled from one studying tactic to another, mirroring the classmates around me who I thought were successful. I was frequently away from campus—in Philadelphia—with wedding-related preparations. And I was *way* behind and extremely anxious all the time.

It was then that I decided to test this "day of rest" theory. If it was a legitimate principle, I needed it now more than ever—even if it felt like not working was the opposite of what I should do. And so from sundown on Saturday to sundown on Sunday, I would do whatever I found restorative and re-creating. For me, that always meant athletics or working out, so I would make sure I went out on a long, slow run where I didn't have to rush out and rush back, or I'd join a series of pickup basketball games at the law school gym. And a Sunday would also involve some

---

* A story for another time, but I wasn't entirely persuaded at the time that all this upheaval was a good idea. I was somewhat convinced by the conviction of my then-fiancé and now-wife, Jean, that this move was a good one, but not entirely. Ultimately, it turned out she was right, which is pretty much always the case!

form of prayer or meditation or worship, most frequently with people but sometimes alone. While in the end I don't know of any effect on my grades (or maybe my grades were beyond help at that stage!) from that semester on, I learned to prioritize what really mattered. As a result, I felt less anxious, more confident, and more comfortable that law school was going to turn out all right one way or another. And it did. In the three decades since that time, I have done my best to take a day of rest. While I haven't kept perfect attendance, so to speak, I've always come back to the practice of rest and reaped the benefits.

The truth is that you and I can always do more; we can always work harder; we can always strive to achieve something greater. There is no ultimate limit. Only you and I can decide when to say, "I've done enough," and "I have enough." This is, ultimately, the only way to prioritize our own rest, recreation, and, most important, renewal.

The most famous businessperson in the twenty-first century is probably Warren Buffett, the famed "Oracle of Omaha" and founder of Berkshire Hathaway, one of the largest and most successful conglomerate holding companies in the world. Buffett has been successful enough that he not only has given away many tens of billions of dollars but also still has many tens of billions of dollars.*

Buffett is nearly as well-known for his wisdom (often shared in folksy ways) as he is for his great wealth and success. Interestingly, eighty-nine-year-old Buffett has spent a life modeling many of these "finding the more in less"principles. After all these years of outsized success, he has not moved from his home in his quiet Omaha neighborhood, which he purchased for $31,500 in 1958, when he was just twenty-eight. Modeling the "I don't need more stuff to be happy" principle, Buffett recently said, "I'm happy there. I'd move if I thought I'd be happier somewhere else."[34] One practice he is famous for is his regular bridge club activities, either at home or at a modest bridge club "studio" in a local Omaha strip mall.[35]

---

*     And although it isn't his money, it is evidence of the success of the company he founded that Berkshire earned $50 billion last year and, as of this writing, has $128 billion in cash.

© Paul Harris/Getty Images

**The (relatively) humble home of one of the
world's richest people, Warren Buffett.**

While I don't know about his "day of rest" principles generally, partici-
pating regularly in the same card-playing ritual over many decades would
seem to imply some quality of recreation and restoration.

And, finally, Buffett is very clear about how he manages his life and
time. With all the demands on him, he learned long ago to set boundaries
for himself and the use of his time. In his own words, "The difference
between successful people and really successful people is that really successful people say no to almost everything."[36] Put another way, no matter
how attractive the possibility, in many cases the best answer when faced
with a variety of choices is to just choose no.

This principle of Sabbath is not just for the religious. In his book *24/6*,
Dr. Matthew Sleeth recounts his family's journey of applying the practice. Dr. Sleeth was a busy emergency room physician and chief of staff
at his hospital when he and his wife, who was also a physician, decided
they had to make a change. Life—the deeper life—was passing them by.
The Sleeths' one rule of thumb for their day of renewal a week provides

a simple runway to begin ushering weekly renewal into our lives: don't do anything that you consider work.

For you this might mean putting your phone in a drawer for the day or putting away your laptop. For others it might mean no chores or phone calls or errands. If you are in school, it might mean no homework. Whatever we consider work—and it's different for each of us—we commit to not doing it for one full day each week. (This is effectively each of us applying Buffett's notion of saying no.) If we apply this practice consistently enough, it just might convince us that what satisfies us most in this life is often already available to us—and that it is comprised of less than we often believe we need.

CHAPTER 4

# YOU WILL FACE ADVERSITY

## REDEEM IT

Serena Burla began running in third grade. By middle school it was clear to her parents and peers that she had a gift. In his insightful book *How Bad Do You Want It?*, award-winning sports journalist Matt Fitzgerald explained that Serena rarely lost a race, and on the rare occasion that it happened, she was inconsolable. By all accounts, she was a winner who was born to run. But by high school, other runners her age seemed to catch up. Serena was good enough each year to make it to the qualifier meet for the Foot Locker Cross Country Championships, but she never placed better than twelfth.

While those results were disappointing to someone with a passion for being a great runner, a small consolation was that her abilities managed to earn her a scholarship at the University of Missouri. Fitzgerald explained that in college "she was again an excellent but not quite outstanding performer, finishing sixth in the NCAA Championship 10,000 meters in her senior season. Having no prospects for a professional running career, she quit the sport after graduating."[1]

In what would seem like another tease from life, a short time later Serena met Isaya Okwiya, a Kenyan American coach of a new post-collegiate running team. Coach Okwiya persuaded Serena to get back into shape and start competing again. The hope reignited her passion, but during Serena's comeback, she noticed a pain in her right hamstring.

Bad news came when she visited her doctor: a cancerous tumor the size of a golf ball had formed on her biceps femoris, one of the three muscles that make up the hamstring.

During Serena's surgery at Memorial Sloan Kettering Cancer Center, Dr. Patrick Boland made the difficult decision to remove not only the cancerous tumor but the entire muscle to which it was attached, leaving Serena with only two hamstring muscles in her right leg. Dr. Boland felt certain she'd be able to walk again, but he wasn't hopeful she'd be able to run again, and certainly not competitively. But something unexpected happened.

When Serena finished her intense rehab, she found that she was able to lift more weight with her bad leg than she could with her good leg. The two muscles were somehow stronger than three. Then she began to run. Her coach noticed that her old mechanics—namely, an unusual outward flare of her right leg—had improved. She'd inexplicably become a more efficient runner. Serena noticed something else; she no longer felt the need to win that she'd embraced since childhood. Instead, she felt joy and gratitude for just being able to run again. The discipline of regular workouts was welcomed, and the discomforts of extreme fatigue and soreness only reminded her that she was making the most of her runs. In other words, her psychology had changed alongside her physiology.

Serena ran the New York City Marathon eight months after the muscle in her right hamstring had been removed. Despite having never competed at that distance before, she finished as the fourth American in a stunning time of 2:37:06. She'd found her stride. In 2017 she became the US national champion at the half-marathon distance, a feat she insists she never would have accomplished without adversity.

Matt Fitzgerald calls what happened in the running career of Serena Burla the "workaround effect." He describes it as the brain's ability to respond to a loss of physical ability by creating new ways to achieve the same (or better) level of performance. "This phenomenon is not confined to sports," he asserts. He points to legendary jazzman Django Reinhardt, who was a virtuoso on the guitar by the time he was eighteen. Then a fire badly burned two fingers on his left hand, leaving them both paralyzed. Reinhardt wasn't deterred. He learned a new way to play that would become known as "hot jazz" and define his legend. "It would very likely never have been born if a loss of physical capacity hadn't challenged Reinhardt to do more with less."[2]

This phenomenon that occurs when we experience a physical setback is known by the medical science community as a form of neuroplasticity. It's a coping mechanism hardwired into all of us that kicks in automatically when a new constraint, like an injury, paralysis, or amputation, affects us physically. But physicians, therapists, and psychologists alike warn that for neuroplasticity to do its magic, another coping skill is needed: adaptability.

In other words, your physiology won't fully adapt to adverse conditions until your psychology does too. If you were to break your leg and simply stew in self-pity while casted and during rehab, you'd likely be left with an atrophied leg that was functionally weaker and less capable than before. This is, after all, the natural course for a broken leg: loss of muscle mass, loss of mobility, loss of strength. And, if you allowed it, loss of confidence in your former capabilities. Studies prove that this natural degeneration will occur unless you effectively change your mind about what that broken leg means.

## Pleasure and Pain

The discussion of how we think about and handle adversity stretches across the landscape of history, from biblical times and antiquity to the coronavirus crisis. While the nuances of opinion and philosophy vary as much as humanity itself, history seems to agree that the presence of adversity at least teaches us about ourselves and, if we are willing to respond in certain ways, shapes us into better people than we would have been without it.

There's no doubt that adversity in its many forms is a part of life. It has shaped the course of history and history's greatest heroes. Who would

Martin Luther King Jr. be if not for his struggles? And Abraham Lincoln, who famously lost nearly every campaign he was in, persevered until he upset conventional wisdom by winning the presidency and helping preserve the Union. Where would this country be if not for the people's will to grow stronger through adversity?

There truly isn't such a thing as a life free of pain, suffering, and loss. While there is no doubt that some face more adversity than others, we all face it nonetheless. It's one of the mysteries—some might say burdens—of life that pleasure and pain coexist, despite our desire only for the former. In other words, what we do with adversity is more nuanced than, for instance, a slogan like Nike's "Just Do It." Perhaps it's best to begin by accepting that the world is a complex mix of pleasure and pain, and somehow, if we are looking, it can point us to our higher purpose.

## Freedom to Choose

Roman emperor Marcus Aurelius shared the view that adversity points us to our higher purpose or, at least, in the right direction. Arguably, the emperor's most famous quote is, "The impediment to action advances action. What stands in the way becomes the way."[3] Said in more common language, Aurelius communicated that *the obstacle is the way*, a modern phrase that is at the heart of the philosophy known as Stoicism.

Aurelius was no stranger to adversity. He lost his wife and every child the two shared except one, the infamous Commodus, who, upon his father's death, went about destroying Aurelius's lifelong work.[4] Epictetus, a famous first-century Greek philosopher who was born a slave, explained that we can learn to distinguish between the circumstances we can control and those we can't.[5] Once we identify the circumstances we can control and we're willing to control them and accept those we can't, adversity can be turned to our advantage.

Lebanese American observer and essayist Nassim Nicholas Taleb offered a more modern spin in his fascinating book *Antifragile*. In it he described a Stoic as "someone who transforms fear into prudence, pain into information, mistakes into initiation, and desire into undertaking."[6] The Stoic philosophy makes an important point about the power of our mind-set.

Still, applying an "obstacle is the way" belief seems easier said than done. Are we supposed to get excited about painful moments in life? Should we celebrate failures as though they were successful? I think this takes it too far and isn't true to who we are as people and how we are wired. Pain is pain, and failure is failure. The point is not to diminish these real and challenging aspects of life but to accept them as unpleasant realities that don't have to diminish us as people. As we discussed in chapter 2, these realities can in fact strengthen us and refine us into the people we are meant to be.

Some adversity, though painful when it happens, can even become comical with the passage of time. I think of the time I lost both front teeth on the Venice Beach basketball courts as an eighteen-year-old. I dove full speed and horizontal to the ground (I was an eager, if not foolish, young player) just when a six-foott-seven, 240-pound former Cleveland State player went for the same loose ball. Biophysical laws required that when his weight landed almost entirely on my head and the first thing hitting the ground were my front teeth, those teeth were going to shatter. And shatter they did, all over the court. It was disconcerting at the time (and it was hard to figure out how to get it all fixed as a young man on the road alone), but soon enough it was merely a good story to share.

I also think of the time I was booed off the Massachusetts GOP state convention stage in April 2018. I was trying to offer the convention attendees a polite concession so everyone could go home early, but many in the audience responded to the message they believed I might try to advance or a negative image they felt I symbolized. They booed so loudly that I wasn't permitted to take the stage. But immediately after the ordeal, I realized I could now handle, and even see the slapstick comedy in, an experience that likely would have dismantled me as a young man.

But adversity can also be deeper and more challenging than a story that becomes better with age. In some cases it takes a long time to find yourself again.

Perhaps the most challenging experience I have had in my entire life was in the period of the seeming dissolution of my marriage to Jean, nearly a decade ago. At that stage of our lives, having been married for nearly twenty years, we had gone through so much together, raising four children (their approximate ages were eight to seventeen at the time this period started) and experiencing all the joys and tribulations that naturally come along with that, building a home that allowed us to broadly extend hospitality, and establishing a wonderful community of mutual friends. She not only was my dear wife and the mother of our children but also had been my best friend in the world for twenty-five years.

Like many things in life—and *everything* in relationships—the issues were complicated. But the gist of it was that Jean felt I wasn't facing my own internal problems, and as a consequence she was unfairly blamed for them. The reality was that I couldn't see her point clearly, and that was very painful for her. As she feared that might not change, she asked that we separate, believing divorce to be the likely outcome. As if that wasn't enough (and I thought that alone was going to kill me), during that same period, my father became gravely ill. It soon became evident that he was destined to die shortly.

As those who have experienced this kind of heartache know, for a while you may not really want to live. In your darkness, you find yourself asking, What's the point, since all I care about seems to have been taken away? In my case, I never thought of taking my own life, but nevertheless, I felt largely indifferent to being alive or dead.

That's why it is critical to live your life with others, which we will discuss in greater detail in chapter 6, "You Are Not Alone." For Jean and me, the saving grace was people—caring for and loving us—who completely sustained us during that period. I couldn't be more grateful for them. I remember a wise friend who sternly (yet justly) pushed me as I kept trying to force solutions to "fix" the problems in my relationship with my wife. What I didn't fully realize at the time was that my wiring to be "Mr. Fix-It"—since the earliest days of my life—may have proved successful in many of my initiatives but was often *very* harmful to Jean. You might think I would see this unhelpful pattern on my own, but as the old saying goes: "If all you have is a hammer, the whole world can seem like a nail." I saw a problem to be fixed, and although my so-called "fixing" was part of the problem, I couldn't find a way to stop the pattern. I stood in this friend's living room, just back from visiting my ill dad and about to leave for a business trip. He pointed out this pattern and asked, "Why can't you stop? What are you afraid will happen if you do?"

I had to leave to catch my flight, but the answer came to me in the middle of a run the next day. I surprised myself as I stopped in tears mid-run and realized I was fundamentally afraid of being alone. As I faced my dad's death at the same time that I was perhaps losing my wife for good, my greatest fear was that I would be alone. I was so afraid of that outcome that I was caught in a self-destructive loop where I was trying to fix the problem because I was afraid of the outcome, but fixing it was part of the problem, which was making things worse. Once I accepted my fear, I was able to find my footing; as a cornerstone of my faith, I knew that the God of my understanding would not leave me[7] and would be sufficient, however painful and terrifyingly uncertain the path ahead might be.

My dad passed soon thereafter, and that was as painful as I feared. But with the loyal assistance of our friends and a lot of work on the most challenging facets of our marriage, Jean and I eventually came back together and within five years were with all those faithful friends in a grand celebration of the twenty-five-year renewal of our wedding vows. While the adversity we experienced was beyond what I had previously thought I could bear, the pain and challenge have been and continue to be redeemed as the years go by. And every minute since that trying time has been richer than all the times that came before it, as we each learned new things about ourselves, about our commitment to each other, and about who we are together.

Renewing my wedding vows with my wife,
best friend, and love of my life, Jean.

The healthiest reaction to adversity is, first, a natural one. Pain. Disappointment. Confusion. Frustration. But once the initial emotion has had its moment, our choice awaits us. In his brilliant book *Man's Search for Meaning*, Austrian neurologist and Holocaust survivor Viktor Frankl reminds us, "Everything can be taken from a man but one thing: the last of the human freedoms—to choose one's attitude in any given set of circumstances."[8]

The question we must ask ourselves in the midst of adversity is this: Do I stay with these natural feelings and let them undo me? Or do I elevate another emotion like hope, courage, or resolve in order to use this adversity to become better than I am now?

"So much of what we hear today about courage is inflated and empty rhetoric that camouflages personal fears about one's likability, ratings, and ability to maintain a level of comfort and status," asserts *Rising Strong* author Brené Brown. "We need more people who are willing to demonstrate what it looks like to risk and endure failure, disappointment, and regret—people willing to feel their own hurt instead of working it out on other people, people willing to own their stories, live their values, and keep showing up."[9]

Ultimately, we need to do more than just accept adversity. Though a healthy response begins there, what makes the difference in our lives is our ability to transform adversity into something other than the natural emotions it initially conjures up. This typically requires an evolution from acceptance to action. History is full of examples of people who have done this, from Joan of Arc to Viktor Frankl, Mahatma Gandhi, Rosa Parks, and Nelson Mandela.

When asked whether she ever grew weary of her stance for civil rights and the volatility that followed it, Rosa Parks responded, "No, the only tired I was, was tired of giving in."[10] She took this thought a bit further when she said, "I have learned over the years that when one's mind is made up, this diminishes fear; knowing what must be done does away with fear."[11]

It's amazing enough that these minds of ours can summon stamina and squash fear by essentially changing the meaning of adversity. But, not to be outdone, our bodies also play a critical role that has been forgotten after decades of modern amenities have kept us from tapping into our deepest capabilities.

In the modern Western world many of us now enjoy, maybe we've forgotten that our bodies are capable of living in nature without big puffy down jackets and other high-tech outerwear. And maybe this understanding will help convince us that we're all-around more capable of handling adversity than we think—not just mentally but physically as well.

## You Are Resilient

In his book *What Doesn't Kill Us*, investigative journalist and anthropologist Scott Carney set out to debunk the legend of a Dutch man named Wim Hof, otherwise known as the "Iceman," who claims that if you give him $2,000 and one week of your life, he will have you sitting outside in snow and Arctic temperatures for hours, in nothing but your underwear, enjoying a conversation as though you're lounging on South Beach in summertime. Hof's claims, as outlandish as they first sound, are based wholly on a theory that you and I can tap into the innate, resilient parts of our physiology that have lain dormant for decades in these controlled environments we now live in—if we are willing to place ourselves in situations that force our bodies' deepest coping mechanisms to kick in.

Carney's book is ultimately about the question of whether today's modern conveniences have killed off the ability humans once had to adapt to the often adverse conditions around us. "The Western-lifestyle makes it all-too-easy to take nature for granted," insists Hof in the foreword of Carney's book. "Sure we can build skyscrapers, fly airplanes and simply turn up the thermostat to combat the cold, but it turns out that the technologies that we believe are our greatest strengths are also our most tenacious crutches. The things we have made to keep us comfortable are making us weak."[12]

Carney admits that he entered the whole ordeal a skeptic. He considered Hof a charlatan, and once he received a commission to write an article about the Iceman, he hopped on a plane to wintry Poland, where Hof's training takes place. In less than twenty-four hours, Carney began to shed his skepticism. Over the week with Hof, he also shed his clothes and joined his fellow trainees in subfreezing temperatures for hours at a time, in a waterfall flanked by icy rocks, in a river studded by snowcapped boulders. He finished the week with a six-hour hike up a 5,200-foot peak in single-digit temperatures and two feet of fresh powder, wearing only hiking boots and shorts. In seven days' time, Carney had traversed "from California palm trees to Poland's snowy peaks," feeling "perfectly warm—hot, even."[13]

Were Hof's methods a link to how much more capable we are in adverse situations? Carney had to know more. After his week in rural Poland, he found himself reflecting on our history and the fact that humans haven't always needed thermostats and heated steering wheels. In 1620 a group of religious outcasts from Europe traveled on rickety ships to the east coast of what is now Massachusetts. It was the middle of winter, and if you've been to the coast of my home state in winter, you know how bitter that cold can be. Imagine the settlers' surprise when a tall indigenous man walked into their camp wearing only a loincloth. He greeted them peacefully, and in return the settlers offered him a fur coat. He took the coat in one hand and shrugged. It turned out that the man's attire—or lack thereof—was standard all-season wear for the Algonquin people. "Their secret didn't rely solely on their genetics," explained Carney. "Contemporary accounts by colonists stated that the local tribes relied on conditioning to make their children more robust. Every winter they placed their infants and children in the snow for a few minutes every day before bringing them back inside their houses. Repeated exposure helped condition the children to become comfortable in environments that would make the typical colonist want to die."[14]

If, as Carney put it, "our ancestors crossed the Alps in animal skins and colonized the New World in loin cloths, seemingly impervious to the elements,"[15] what has happened to us modern humans? Have we lost something intrinsic to our beings? In our air-conditioned homes, under the glow of our HD lights, do we underestimate an innate inner strength that allows us to turn challenging circumstances into something natural, if not supernatural? And if that's true, how do we become more conditioned to handle adversity the way our ancestors did?

Is the secret, as Wim Hof's methods demonstrate, in our physiology? Or is the secret, as the Stoics believed, in our psychology?

Stories like those of Serena Burla, Scott Carney, and Viktor Frankl remind us that the real secret to addressing adversity in the best way is a combination of both mind and body. But there's another secret too. It's found in the stories themselves.

## You Are a Redemption Story

Dan McAdams, a psychologist at Northwestern University, has dedicated decades to studying the effect of personal narratives, or the stories we tell ourselves about our own lives. In particular, his work focuses on the power of what he calls "redemption stories" that make up the "quintessentially American story about how to live a good life."[16] Such stories, explains McAdams, contain five themes:

1. "Early advantage," or becoming aware of our unique gifts.
2. "Sensitivity to suffering," or noticing the pain, suffering, and injustice in the world.
3. "Moral steadfastness," or determining to live according to a firm sense of right and wrong.
4. "Redemption sequences," or making significant mistakes or suffering hardships and finding a way to turn them into an "enhanced state."
5. "Prosocial goals," or using what we've learned from our own adversity to improve the lives of others.[17]

To explore the possible significance of a personal redemption story, McAdams and his colleague Jen Guo interviewed 157 middle-aged adults for two to three hours, asking each to describe his or her life as if it were a novel with chapters, characters, and themes.

When McAdams and Guo studied their interviewees' stories, they found that those who had redemptive personal narratives also lived lives of what McAdams calls "generativity," which is characterized by generosity, selflessness, and a desire to make the world a better place not just for themselves but for others too. In his previous work, McAdams showed that generativity is directly tied to better parenting, better community engagement, better mental health, and lower incidence of depression.

Does this mean that if we see our stories as redemptive or see that the arc of the moral universe, in the words popularized by Martin Luther King Jr., "bends toward justice,"[18] we will suffer through less adversity than others or in some way not feel the full brunt of pain, anger, and disappointment? Not at all. What it means is that when we see our lives on a redemptive arc, we are better prepared to accept that adversity is part of life and are more prone to do all we can to ensure that adversity becomes a lesson or even a positive, life-changing event.

In *The Lessons of History*, the concise survey of the culture and civilization of humanity, Pulitzer Prize and Presidential Medal of Freedom winners Will and Ariel Durant remind us, "If we . . . ask what determines whether a challenge will or will not be met, the answer is that this depends upon the presence or absence of initiative and of creative individuals with clarity of mind and energy of will . . . capable of effective responses to new situations. . . . In any case a challenge successfully met (as by the United States in 1917, 1933, and 1941) . . . raises the temper and level of a nation, and makes it abler to meet further challenges."[19]

*How I think about and respond to adversity affects you. And how you think about and respond to adversity affects me.* While I don't intend for that message to be as didactic as that might sound, I think it's important to note that when you or I navigate something difficult (like the coronavirus crisis) with authenticity and hope, it can have a positive impact on more than just our individual lives. Your redemption story can change how I view my story. My redemption story can change how another person views their story. Eventually, if enough of us perceive life through a redemptive lens, the larger challenges of society and the world can come into more meaningful focus. Shame, anger, and blame will be replaced by hope, humanity, and the anticipation of healing. This is the domino effect of one meaningful response to adversity. It first reminds us that we aren't alone in our pain, confusion, and suffering. Then it shows us that adversity is not the end of the story; there is a way forward, and redemption can be found. Imagine what can happen when this spirit pervades an entire country.

If we look, we might see that it's already happening around us.

Jake Wood was a football player in his freshman year at the University of Wisconsin when the attacks of September 11, 2001, occurred. Like many, he felt the tug to do something in response. He was riveted when nine months later professional football player Pat Tillman announced his sudden retirement to enlist in the US Army and serve our country in the war on terror. When Jake learned of Tillman's tragic death by friendly fire in Khost Province, Afghanistan, less than two years later, he was concluding his senior year at Wisconsin. In a private moment of reflection, he decided to act on a conviction that had been building in his spirit for years. He enlisted in the Marines after college graduation and served as a scout sniper on the battlefields of Iraq and Afghanistan, eventually concluding his four years as a decorated sergeant in 2009. When a devastating earthquake struck Haiti three months later, Jake was still struggling to navigate civilian life after war. As he watched the horrific images of Port-au-Prince scroll across his TV screen, he knew he had something he could offer to the Haitian people in perhaps their greatest time of need. He rallied a group of eight veterans and doctors to join him in a rogue effort to deliver aid to the survivors in Port-au-Prince.

While the effort wasn't about the men on the mission, Jake realized in Haiti that his ragtag relief effort not only was serving the devastated Haitian people but also was giving him and his fellow vets a sense of purpose they'd been searching for since returning home from war. In the months that followed his return to the States, Jake founded Team Rubicon with a small cohort of friends and former Marines. The idea was simple: recruit, train, and deploy military veterans—who are experienced in effectively responding to adversity—to respond to natural disasters and humanitarian crises at home and abroad. In doing so, both those suffering under disaster and those struggling through the complexities of returning home from war could find redemption.

Since 2010, Team Rubicon has grown from its original eight volunteers to over one hundred thousand strong. To date they have responded to more than three hundred disasters around the globe, like the 2011 tornado in Joplin, Missouri; Hurricane Sandy in 2012; the 2013 Typhoon Haiyan in the Philippines; and Hurricane Harvey in 2017. The team's service in the midst of adversity has been so effective that *Outside* magazine declared that "the future of disaster relief isn't the Red Cross."[20]

In 2018, Jake Wood took the stage at ESPN's annual ESPY Awards to accept the Pat Tillman Award for Service. He concluded his brief but powerful acceptance speech with the following thoughts that I hope will echo for decades to come:

> We have a saying at Team Rubicon: If Americans treated each other every day like they do after disasters, we'd live in a truly special place.
>
> Our nation's capacity to love our neighbors is near limitless after a Category 5 hurricane. We donate, we serve, and we pray. Citizens cross the proverbial train tracks to help those they wouldn't speak to the day prior. But why is it in the months following a storm, we retreat back into our corners to dismiss the human beings that we'd come to love just weeks prior?
>
> We can do better, and we must do better. Know your neighbor, love your neighbor, help your neighbor. Doing that is the best thing for our country right now.[21]

When adversity comes, we've been uniquely equipped to redeem it both individually and together.

# CHAPTER 5

# YOU NEED PEOPLE

## ENGAGE IN PERSON

This is what our brains were wired for," wrote Matthew Lieberman in the book *Social,* "reaching out to and interacting with others. These social adaptations are central to making us the most successful species on earth."[1] Lieberman, an award-winning social psychologist, uses modern MRI technology to demonstrate how our brains seem to prioritize connection and harmony with others to the point that the greatest pleasure and pain we feel is directly tied to our engagement with others.

For example, we can likely understand why we feel some pleasure in getting a large and unexpected gift of cash, however short-lived that might be. But why is it that we experience similar pleasure when giving away money? And why is the emotional pain of being left out of a game of catch so similar to the pain of a physical injury?

In short, it's because our brains are wired to dwell on relationships, for better or worse.

While we've certainly all felt the highs of being accepted and valued as well as the lows of being rejected and devalued, Lieberman's research indicates that these responses are more than fleeting feelings to be celebrated or toughed out. For instance, Lieberman's images show that our brains' pain centers respond less demonstratively when we're in the presence of loved ones. Pain, in other words, is less painful when we're with close friends and family.

Our brains even dwell on relationships in default mode, when at rest.

As an illustration, if a person is asked to do math problems, with a minute between calculations, neuroscientists know that the prefrontal cortex of the brain is active during the math work. But what happens when the person's brain is at rest? What is its "default" mode? Interestingly, we think about one another. For example, I might wonder whether I was too harsh during my last email exchange or whether a potential new friend was also interested in friendship with me. I might think about my sons' well-being or my daughters' activities. I might think about coworkers and whether they understand what I'm trying to do with my work.

Why would the brain's default mode go to relationships? Lieberman tells us that these relationships are more important than we understand. Our brain's default system "allows us to figure out the psychological characteristics of the people we see every day so we can better predict their reactions to novel situations and avoid unnecessary feather ruffling."[2]

While Lieberman describes this phenomenon from a neuroscientific framework, the great Jewish philosopher and theologian Martin Buber used another approach to describe the magic that exists between human beings when we are connected with each other. "When two people relate to each other authentically and humanly," he wrote, "God is the electricity that surges between them."[3]

This "electricity" is almost mystical, because it doesn't look like much to the naked eye. If it were filmed, the camera might not even pick it up at all. Yet if we believe Lieberman and Buber, connecting with one another is at the core of who we are. Given our isolation experiences as a consequence of the "stay at home" and "shelter in place" mandates in the coronavirus period—and how much people generally crave in-person human connection!—we may all find ourselves more inclined to believe that Lieberman and Buber are, in fact, on to something.

## How We Got Here

I launched my travels across the country on a late summer day in 1983 as my Greyhound bus pulled out of the Hartford, Connecticut, bus station.

My mother waved goodbye knowing that we would have the most limited of interaction over the next year—perhaps an occasional letter (though they weren't much for correspondence) or a call on a holiday, but not much beyond that. Nearly 100 percent of my human interaction over the better part of the next year would be in person, with people I met along the way. This was the normal course of engaging with others, not just when I was seventeen but for thousands of years before then.

Until the advent of the printing press in the 1400s, there was no true method of mass communication, if it can even be called that by today's standards. It wasn't until five hundred years later that the radio came along, and the television not long after that. But when digital messaging via the internet became widely available in the 1990s, our communication with one another could transcend the barriers of time, space, and economics. It offered, for the first time ever, nearly complete and full-time connectivity.

I recall a staggering glimpse of this future when I stayed with new friends on the campus of Stanford University in April 1984. I had first met these Stanford undergrads only days into my trip the year before.* I don't have any idea how I contacted them once I made my way to their neck of the woods eight months later—I guess it must have been by pay phone. Nevertheless, when I stepped into the dorm room of my West Coast friends, I noticed a remarkable new machine on their desk. It looked different from anything I had ever seen. Yes, it was the iconic Apple Macintosh, the first computer truly designed for people who were not technology "geeks."

It was approximately a decade later, in the mid-1990s, when emails spread beyond the earliest adopters, and humanity's latest wave of "not in person" interaction started. However, this new virtual communication was limited because email was accessible only by computers, which for most people happened only when they were at work. (Or occasionally

---

\*     We met in line at Rockefeller Center in September 1983 as we waited to see then–breakout star David Letterman on his new show, *Late Night with David Letterman.*

when they "dialed up" a connection from home—so sluggish, so slow, so easy to be bounced offline!)

All that changed in January 2007, when Steve Jobs stepped onstage at Macworld. Jobs teased his adoring audience by announcing he was introducing three revolutionary devices:

- a widescreen iPod with touch controls
- a revolutionary mobile phone
- a breakthrough internet communications device

As you have probably guessed by now, Jobs was in fact introducing just one extraordinary device called the iPhone. The legendary device leapfrogged all the so-called "smartphones" of the day and put the power of avoiding in-person human contact in the hands of everyone who could afford it.

In the thirteen years since, nearly everyone has some form of smartphone in their purse or pocket or, more likely, in their hands. And with that, they now have the ability to ignore and avoid in-person human contact at nearly every moment of every day, if they so choose.

The iPhone was revolutionary and extraordinary indeed. Magnificent in its scope, mind-blowing in its capacity. But if its use is not checked, it can be completely lethal to meaningful human interaction. I often say the smartphone can be a weapon of mass relationship destruction. Not literally and physically, of course, but certainly psychologically and spiritually.

The bad news is that we have technology that we don't fully appreciate how to use.

The good news is that having named the challenge, we can and will overcome it.

News innovator Jim VandeHei founded two of the most significant "new news" businesses of recent decades, first POLITICO and then more recently Axios. VandeHei observed:

> We're still very adolescent in our usage of these really cool technologies, which if used right, can be transformative in a very positive way.

If abused, they could really grind up and grind down our country. We are still pretty irresponsible in our usage of them—not just our kids; we're irresponsible in our use of them. My guess is over time, we figure out better boundaries and different ways to put either government regulation or self-regulation around it.[4]

Setting the "abuse" and "grind up and grind down" of VandeHei's comments into what are perhaps more recognizable terms, consider the relatively familiar modern scenario of someone who sits in a room alone (even apart from "social distancing" protocols) and whiles away many hours bingeing Netflix and at the same time scanning the world of social media.

I have nothing against Netflix (I personally love long-form dramatic series), and social media is cool in so many ways. Retreating from the world for periods, and in moderation, is good. I also appreciate that some of us are wired a little differently and need a little less interaction. For most of us, however, if Netflix bingeing and social media interactions are a complete replacement for tangible relationships, our chances of experiencing the fulfillment and electricity described by Lieberman and Buber aren't very high.

As we try to navigate our way back to real human connection and create the right boundaries for our use of these magnificent technologies, there are three key dimensions to consider.

One is the cost of being "absent" from the human beings immediately around us. In effect, snubbing our friends and loved ones and instead paying attention to our phones—what some now call "phubbing."

The second is the cost of trying to get real relationship sustenance through digital devices, which I'll explain as the "Twinkie" problem.

The third is the cost of inevitable misunderstanding, large and small, when we communicate across the digital world, which we might refer to as the "telephone game" issue.

## Ignoring Your Friends and Loved Ones

We are prewired for real, human connection with others. Connection is the pinnacle of our existence. And yet nearly all of us carry with us everywhere something that can transport us anywhere on the planet in seconds. And when transported to that other place, we aren't fully where we are. According to recent statistics, the average person touches their phone over 2,600 times a day.[5]

In 2014 researchers from Virginia Tech released a report called "The iPhone Effect: The Quality of In-Person Social Interactions in the Presence of Mobile Devices." For their study, the researchers observed one hundred couples engaged in ten-minute conversations, with and without cell phones present. Besides the obvious distraction the presence of the phones brought on, the researchers noted that the phones' presence fed "a constant urge to seek out information, check for communication, and direct their thoughts to other people and worlds. . . . Their mere presence in a socio-physical milieu, therefore, has the potential to divide consciousness between the proximate and immediate setting and the physically distant and invisible networks and contexts."[6]

The researchers used some dense and complicated words to say something that is fairly obvious to anyone in the modern age. With a phone around, we often ignore the person we are with to pursue a distraction from somewhere else in the world, leaving the person through what is effectively a digital transporter. Imagine you were sitting with someone you cared deeply about, and instead of the 2,600 phone touches in a day, in each of those 2,600 cases, that person suddenly and without explanation turned their back and looked the other way for a few seconds. It would throw off the quality of your connection, wouldn't it?

Obviously, the scenario isn't that stark, because we probably couldn't get away with turning our backs on our friends and loved ones 2,600 times a day. But the idea isn't wholly different either.

I have a confession to make. Nearly two decades ago, my job with my technology-forward company prompted me to be a very early adopter

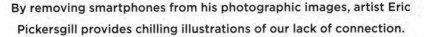

**By removing smartphones from his photographic images, artist Eric Pickersgill provides chilling illustrations of our lack of connection.**

of the first-generation smartphone, the BlackBerry. The culture of my company was such that we were generally "on the clock" all the time, which meant that wherever I might go, whatever time of day or night it was, I would be ready to roll with my handy BlackBerry. Because I was eager to show my worth to my ambitious teammates, I allowed the device to disrupt the rhythm of my family life. It was unsettling to have my wife or family comment on my approach, and I was defensive about it for a long time. (You can probably imagine the defense I used—"But this is for work.") In what may have been a "window into the soul" of our family—and at minimum was a really amusing moment—my youngest child, William, dumped my BlackBerry into the toilet. Not once, not twice, but three times!

In the early days, the smartphone was still unusual enough that everyone would talk about how odd these machines were (many derisively called them "crackberries" because of their addictive qualities). When spouses of my colleagues gathered, they would commiserate with one another about our peculiar work habits and how disruptive our use of these devices was to our family lives.

What has happened since then? This behavior, which nearly all recognized as wildly disruptive and antisocial in its early days when displayed by these small outlier bands (like me and my teammates), has become the norm.

Once upon a time, not too long ago, we all recognized that constantly having our noses in our phones was weird behavior and would dump the devices of offenders like me into the toilet. Now most people have smartphones and seem to have given each other a collective "hall pass" to disrupt family rhythms and ignore our friends and loved ones a lot more than we ought to.

## The Twinkie Problem

The first Twinkie was made in 1930, and Twinkies have been a part of American pop culture ever since. So fabled were the oblong golden sponge cakes that President Bill Clinton included Twinkies in the 1999 millennium time capsule as an illustration of pop culture of the era.

Bottom line, whether or not you love those sponge cakes with creamy vanilla filling, one thing everyone knows: they aren't healthy! Packed with processed sugar and empty calories, there is even a long-standing urban legend that Twinkies never decompose and have an infinite shelf life (perhaps explaining Clinton's choice to include one in a time capsule).

If you start with a healthy and balanced diet of proteins, vegetables, and other nutrients your body needs to thrive, the Twinkie is a perfectly fine "final" item to consume. If you eat a good moderate meal, and the Twinkie is your dessert of choice, then go for it! However, if you eat nothing but Twinkies for weeks, months, or years, your system won't function the way it is supposed to; I'm not smart enough to say exactly what the physical effects will be, but I do know they won't be good. While your body may want Twinkies, it doesn't need Twinkies; it needs real nutrients.

For me, social media and digital communities are a lot like the Twinkie. Only in unusual cases and for short periods of time will devouring online connections (without real in-person ones) fill you up.

Let's start with the first problem—these connections are rarely authentic and honest.

It is hard to imagine a better illustration of this than the widely reported lake in Novosibirsk, Siberia, which is frequented by visitors posting on social media. The pristine turquoise hue of this lake, nicknamed the "Siberian Maldives," is the product of chemical reactions between toxic waste elements from a local power station. It is here, with water saturated with heavy metals and harmful substances, that thousands of visitors—ranging from vacationers in their bathing suits to newlywed couples—have been regularly Instagramming.[7] Despite expert warnings that the lake can cause chemical burns or other reactions if ingested or touched, people venture out to its bright blue for their picturesque selfies. People enter actual toxic wastelands so that people online believe they are in an exotic paradise.

**Taking pictures at the toxic "Siberian Maldives" lake.**

Though clearly most don't go to the extreme of presenting a toxic dump as a slice of their own paradise, we can easily imagine how we can fall into presenting similarly false realities. Imagine someone (let's call him Ryan) who chooses not to digitally share the six days in a row in which he has struggled with family conflict or job insecurity, but then on the seventh day, he has a good outing. Ryan goes to an interesting event or has a magnificent meal with family or friends, and that seems sufficiently "grammable" or "gramworthy" (or the Facebook, Snapchat, or TikTok equivalent), and so Ryan snaps the picture, adds a clever description (#blessed, anyone?), and posts it.

Is that one picture of Ryan's life a lie? Of course not; it did actually happen. But the two good hours were cherry-picked out of the 168-hour week and weren't an authentic presentation of the week Ryan had. Most of us have an understandable desire to show the rosy versions of our lives, as Ryan did, with little incentive to show the tough days because, honestly, who wants to publicly share the problems and challenges of our lives? The knock-on effect is that the receiving audience believes, just a touch more, that this is the baseline for how we all live. *See how good Ryan's life is?* (Not seeing the other 166 hours of Ryan's week.) *Why can't my life be more like Ryan's?*

Wash. Rinse. Repeat. Because nearly everyone makes the same social media judgment that Ryan made, hundreds of millions and billions of such messages get conveyed. Somehow, in a modern world in which anxiety and depression and loneliness are experienced in record numbers, if we view only our social media and digital lives, we are led to believe there are very few problems at all.

A second key problem is that many of us don't hold ourselves suitably accountable or responsible, given that we feel veiled in the digital world.

One extreme example of this is Discord, which has become popular as a round-the-clock conversational platform built around the up-all-night culture of gaming. Because it is used largely by gamers, the principal demographic is—you guessed it—adolescent boys. Discord, unlike other digital forums, echoes a key element of in-person engagement: real-time interaction and discourse.[8] Super cool? Absolutely. But what is often experienced on Discord is not super cool.

On Discord, teens are anonymously registered and effectively unsupervised, which, as you might imagine, gives rise to a host of problems. As the mother of one Discording boy has observed, "These kids are not calling, texting or Skyping each other anymore. They're all just Discording. The going sentence between kids is 'Go Kill Yourself.' I hate it."[9]

Now, we all appreciate that teenage boys are their own breed, but strip away the extra drama and intensity of teenage male life, and you see some themes we can all identify with. In-person engagement can't happen anonymously. We have to be accountable and responsible to one another because we are wired to be that way with real human beings. But when online, we can imagine away the humanity of our online counterpart and see them merely as an avatar of something we don't like or respect or understand, and therefore we largely don't hold ourselves to the same standard as we would in person.

This lack of online accountability and responsibility can reach tragic dimensions. One example is Desmond Amofah, who was found dead in New York's East River in June 2019. Amofah had risen to social media stardom, attaining hundreds of thousands of followers and subscribers through his YouTube gaming channel. His online behavior became erratic in October 2018, as he shared suicidal messages, slurs, and pornography. Then, in April 2019, nearly twenty thousand people watched as he livestreamed a seeming suicide attempt from his bedroom window.[10] Police eventually drilled through his door and he was hospitalized. Later calling into the YouTube gossip show *DramaAlert*, Amofah continued to demonstrate symptons of mental illness. The host of the show, Keemstar, seemingly taunted him: "If you really think about it, then why live? Just jump off a cliff?" Days later, Amofah effectively did just that.

Amofah left a YouTube suicide "note" sharing his wish that his story would "make YouTube a better place, somehow, in the future, to where people know boundaries and limits to how far things should go."[11]

Amofah's mental illness challenges clearly were not caused by the internet and social media alone. And, of course, callousness like Keemstar's is not new to our age. But while extreme, it does point to a fundamental reality of the digital age—we aren't typically as responsible and accountable to our online "friends" as we are to our real ones.

## The Telephone Game

Engaging one another in person is no longer the norm. It's now the exception. The conveniences of our many forms of communication have made us far more productive in many respects and have certainly made it easier for us to stay connected to anyone just about anywhere on earth. But over the last two decades, we've traded a regimen of healthy (even if hard) face-to-face conversations for a cacophony of digital discourse that often fails to convey the full meaning behind our messages and creates misunderstanding and offense.

In the opening of Dale Carnegie's classic 1936 bestseller, *How to Win Friends and Influence People,* his seminal statement is simply: "Dealing with people is probably the biggest problem you face."[12] In the modern update of the classic, we're reminded that while our relationships are still our biggest blessing and toughest challenge, a lot has changed in how we connect with one another today. "Messaging speed is instantaneous. Communication media have multiplied. Networks have expanded beyond borders, industries, and ideologies. . . . If you don't begin with the right foundation, it is easy to send the wrong message, to offend, or to fall embarrassingly short of your objective."[13]

Perhaps this rising tension we feel isn't so much about the words we're using or the posture we're taking. The real issue is that we just don't engage in person like we used to, and therefore the real meaning of what we try to communicate is lost in translation.

"We live in a driven, digital world where the full value of human connection is often traded for transactional proficiency," asserts Carnegie and Associates. "Many have mastered the ironic art of increasing touch points while simultaneously losing touch."[14]

It's easy to see how misinterpretation, frustration, and anger have risen. We've largely removed the core ingredients of understanding, empathy, and collaboration from our conversations.

"As a communication medium, face-to-face interaction is information-rich," wrote Carol Kinsey Goman, body language expert and author of *The Silent Language of Leaders*. "People are interpreting the meaning of what you say only partially from the words you use. They get most of your message (and all the emotional nuance behind the words) from vocal tone, pacing, facial expressions and body language."[15]

In his famous 1971 book, *Silent Messages*, Albert Mehrabian, one of the fathers in the study of nonverbal communication, introduced a still-widely-accepted equation that breaks down the level of impact our words, our tone, and our facial cues have on communicating our feelings about a message that's shared with us. He explained: "Total feeling = 7% verbal feeling + 38% vocal feeling + 55% facial feeling." In other words, if we like what we've heard, or others like what we've communicated, our facial expressions "will dominate and determine the impact of the total message."[16] Said another way, if we remove physical presence from conversation, we remove more than half of our ability to accurately convey our messages to one another. If we're just reading words on a screen, our interpretations are being made without 93 percent of the information we need to confirm a message.

———

The body of research now suggests that such digital disconnects don't occur only because we're missing the critical information provided by verbal tone and nonverbal cues; we also overestimate our ability to convey our intended tone through virtual communication *and* our ability to correctly interpret the intended tone of others. This egocentric tendency was highlighted in a 2006 study conducted by New York University professor Justin Kruger and University of Chicago professor and *Mindwise* author Nicholas Epley.

In the study, sixty Cornell students were instructed, individually and privately, to select ten messages from a list of twenty that they felt would be simplest for another person to decipher between a serious or sarcastic tone. The students were then paired up, and one member of each pair was asked to type the messages they selected into an email. The other member of each pair was asked to read their ten messages into an audio recorder. All sixty students were then individually asked about their confidence in their messages being interpreted correctly by their partner. Of the students who had emailed the messages, 78 percent were confident that their messages would be accurately interpreted as serious or sarcastic. Of the students who had recorded the messages, 78 percent also felt confident that their messages would be interpreted accurately. In other words, nearly eight out of ten students in both scenarios were confident that their messages would be accurately understood, regardless of the medium of communication. The results told a different story.

Whereas 73 percent of the students interpreting the audio messages were correct, only half the students interpreting the email messages were correct, leading Kruger and Epley to conclude that the latter students' accuracy in interpreting the digital messages was "indistinguishable from chance."[17] This overconfidence in our digital communication has since been observed in similar studies.[18]

You wouldn't be surprised to know that researchers have found that the fewer cues we have to verify the meaning of our words in various forms of communication, the less we're able to bond with each other. A study conducted by three UCLA psychology professors showed that to the degree a communications medium reduces the availability of physical and verbal cues (facial expression, voice tone, nods, smiles, etc.), our level of bonding decreases. The researchers tested fifty-eight young women, recruited in pairs of close friends, and asked them to engage in four conversations each, via different mediums of communication: in person, video chat, audio chat, and instant messaging (aka texting and direct messaging). The participants' level of bonding in each condition was measured through both self-reported interviews that followed the conversations and what the researchers call "affiliation cues," or "non-verbal behaviors associated with the emotional experience of bonding."

The results?

"Participants reported feeling connected in all conditions. However, bonding, as measured by both self-report and affiliation cues, differed significantly across conditions, with the greatest bonding during in-person interaction, followed by video chat, audio chat, and IM in that order."[19]

The following chart illustrates the sharp decrease in affiliate bonding cues that occured when the participants moved from in-person conversation (the highest) down to text messaging (the lowest). (The numbers below are a composite score based on the frequency of smiles and head nods over the course of the conversation and the total number of seconds during which laughter and gestures were identified.)

When you consider how much of today's communication takes place through mediums that are not only void of the most important elements of understanding but also largely taking place in a one-way fashion where there really isn't an active conversation, it's easy to see how so much disconnection and misunderstanding occur.

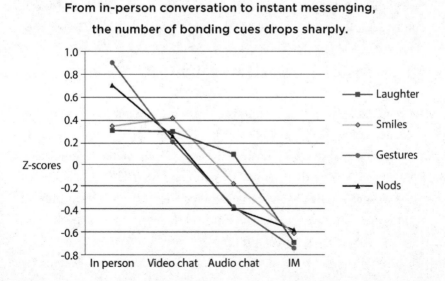

**From in-person conversation to instant messenging, the number of bonding cues drops sharply.**

In short, today's advances in communication have increased our connectivity while decreasing our quality of connection.

This reminds me of the telephone game that's been around forever. You know it, right? A group of people gather in a circle or around a table or room, and someone starts the game by whispering a random phrase, like "LeBron James is on the Lakers," in the ear of the person next to them. That person then whispers what they heard to the next person, and around the room the message goes until the last person announces the message they heard: "Candy canes have no haters." More often than not, the final message is so far off base from the original message that it is pretty funny.

It feels like we're playing a massive game of telephone today. Only the translations aren't funny; they're often hurtful.

## The Pros Have Figured It Out

A September 2019 *Business Insider* headline almost shouts a key insight at us: "Bill Gates and Steve Jobs raised their kids tech-free—and it should've been a red flag."[20] Author Allana Akhtar pointed to the work of educators Joe Clement and Matt Miles, who argued that it is telling that two of the most important technology figures in history—Gates and Jobs—rarely allowed their children to use the products they created. Clement and Miles asked, "What is it these wealthy tech executives know about their own products that their consumers don't?"[21]

These were among the examples Akhtar cited:

- Gates didn't allow his kids to get cell phones until they were fourteen, and he implemented a cap on screen time for his children.
- Jobs prohibited his kids from using the iPad, saying in a 2011 interview, "We limit how much technology our kids use at home."[22]
- Snapchat CEO Evan Spiegel and his wife, Miranda Kerr, impose a ninety-minute screen time limit on their children *per week.*

Obviously, the rules aren't the same for children as for adults, but

© Rob Latour/Shutterstock

**Bill Gates and his daughter Jennifer.**

these relatively strict examples are suggestive of some principles that are relevant for all of us. The key is imposing boundaries and setting limits on ourselves so our various digital worlds are positioned in the right place in our lives.

Another technology pro who gets the importance of old-school, in-person communication is Ronald Ly, head coach of UCI Esports teams. If you were to ask me to choose one area in life where the old "in-person is best" rules don't hold any longer, it would be esports or, as it is often more casually described, gaming. In a recent interview, Ly shared the surprising insight that he directs his players to spend a lot of time playing, and many hours as a team, *in a room together*! Ly observes that a key barrier to the progress of many players in gaming is that they lack the "social skills or relational abilities to elevate their play above a surface level."[23] To remedy that, Ly brings his collegiate-level teams together to practice thirty hours a week, with premeetings, scrimmages, and postscrimmage debriefings where they discuss as a team whether they hit their goals for the day and what went well.

Another recent illustration of the emerging understanding of this "in person" principle is the Texas Tech 2018–2019 men's basketball team. The Red Raiders had lost five of their top six scorers from the prior successful season, one that had culminated in a long run in the NCAA tournament, making it through to the Elite Eight. Because the team was stripped of the core players from the previous season and had few (if any) high-level new recruits, most observers had very low expectations for the upcoming season.

Against that backdrop, coach Chris Beard took his team away for a two-day preseason retreat. Upon arrival, as they stepped off the bus, the players were asked to surrender their phones so they could spend the next forty-eight hours fully present with one another. Coach Beard assigned them questions to ask each other about where they had come from and what motivated them, and they then shared their findings with the rest of the team. Like my son and the other young men in the wilderness therapy program, all the players had was each other.

The Texas Tech team went on to have the most successful season in school history, proceeding to the NCAA championship game where they stretched Tony Bennett's UVA squad to overtime before falling in an epic finale. One sportswriter observed that the preseason retreat "transformed a loosely connected group of basketball players into a tightly bonded team capable of making history."[24] Of course, the retreat wasn't the only factor. The supremely talented Jarrett Culver (now with the Minnesota Timberwolves) and a lot of other good players, plus terrific execution, figured meaningfully in this success. But Coach Beard and the Red Raiders honored the very important "in person" principle, and it was an undeniable contributor to the team's success.[25]

## One at a Time, Human to Human

Anchored by our understanding of who we are and the developing understanding of how to rein in the increasingly obvious costs of these technologies, we can and will figure this out.

The only way to do that is to start small, one conversation at a time. As MIT professor Sherry Turkle observed in her landmark book *Reclaiming Conversation*, "Face-to-face conversation is the most human—and humanizing—thing we do. Fully present to one another, we learn to listen. It's where we develop the capacity for empathy."[26]

This principle can sound old-fashioned, especially when it comes packaged as it does in the Robert Frost poem "A Time to Talk":

> When a friend calls to me from the road
> And slows his horse to a meaning walk,
> I don't stand still and look around
> On all the hills I haven't hoed,
> And shout from where I am, What is it?
> No, not as there is a time to talk.
> I thrust my hoe in the mellow ground,
> Blade-end up and five feet tall,
> And plod: I go up to the stone wall
> For a friendly visit.[27]

While few of us experience a life with horses and hoes and hills to cultivate, we still need to prioritize other people and conversations. Maybe the "hoe" we need to thrust into the ground looks more like a smartphone today?

A clever commercial for the 2020 Nissan Altima begins with a shot of a young professional man in his urban-style loft reading a text on his phone. He ponders the message while gazing out the window where he sees his Altima at the curb on the street below. He checks his watch and heads to his car. The camera then follows his car as he cruises under a bridge and past city buildings as the light outside turns from dusk to evening and the neon sign of a restaurant comes to life. In the final shot, we see the young man knocking on the door of a house in a suburban neighborhood. The door opens, and we see another young man inside, a little surprised at the man standing in his doorway.

"Are you answering my text in person?" the homeowner asks.

"I am, yeah," says the man outside with a grin.

"Come on in," the homeowner, clearly a friend, replies.[28]

Let's set down our modern "hoe" equivalents and use our modern "horse" equivalents to respond to one another in person, whenever and wherever possible.

———

As life circumstances change over time, the application of important principles needs to adapt as well. I have been pretty committed to the "I need people—engage in person" principle but recently realized that as my life had changed in recent years, I needed to figure out new ways to approach this. In my case, I reflected on the fact that my regular "hang out" friend had moved to another city; my campaign had ended and, with it, seven-day-a-week engagement; and my children were no longer competing in their many sports, so I wasn't seeing other parents on the sidelines anymore. I felt alone, and the people I had spent the most time with in person were from a chapter of life that was now past. So what now?

I recalled a concept I tried to instill in my children (to their chagrin). In our family we call it "neighborhood friends." It's a concept that may seem foreign or strange in the age of *Fortnite* and streaming video entertainment. Neighborhood friends are the friends who usually live within walking distance from home, whether in the house next door or at the end of your street. They are friends who at any given moment might knock on your door asking if you want to go for a bike ride or play soccer in the street. Our neighborhood friends could become some of our most meaningful and cherished relationships.

So I made a decision: I would go knock on the doors of my neighbors and check in with them or ask them if they wanted to hang out with me. Admittedly, I didn't know my neighbors well. Because our children were different ages or we moved into the neighborhood at different times, or any other variant in our life rhythms, my neighbors and I never had reason nor made the extra effort to connect. Aside from the polite greetings and distant waves, we were, in some cases, largely strangers. But maybe just like the neighborhood friends of my youth, it would take only a knock.

To set the stage, it was seven at night in early winter in New England, meaning it had been pitch-black for hours already. Temperatures were in the low thirties. The elements were not encouraging me in my efforts.

My first knock was at the door of a man whom we will call Greg, whose porch light was off. He and I were not total strangers—our paths had crossed years earlier when I had connected him with resources to help him through a challenging marital situation, and occasionally we texted. Since then, however, we had lost touch.

With a look of surprise, Greg greeted me at his front door and then stepped outside in the dark to greet me.

"Hey, Greg!" I said as unawkwardly as I could. "I know it has been a while, but I thought I would come by, say hello, and see how you are doing."

Within a matter of minutes, Greg proceeded to open up his life to me, sharing some of his most painful moments from the past year. Fifteen minutes later, we shared a warm embrace on his front porch. I was shocked and overwhelmed. I had certainly not expected this and was blown away by his wonderful and open heart.

The following morning, I received a text from Greg, thanking me for knocking on his door the evening before. He expressed how grateful he was, and even though we had not spoken in some time, my standing with him on that porch in the dark and cold, listening to him, and embracing him as a friend meant a great deal.

After saying good night to Greg the night before, I had made my way across the street to the home of a young couple named Jack and Diane (more aliases, if you didn't guess) and their children. Unlike with Greg, my path had hardly ever crossed with that of Jack and Diane (our children were much different ages), but when we spoke briefly on rare occasions, I imagined really liking them.

When I knocked on their door, they were even more surprised than Greg had been.

"Hi, can we help you?" they asked.

For a second time that evening, I shared my desire to simply say hello and, in this case, asked whether they wanted to hang out sometime. To my surprise, they told me they would love to and asked whether I could return in a short while since they were putting their children to bed.

I came back later that evening to find them awaiting my return with a freshly opened bottle of wine. Although I had picked up my own take-out Chinese food (they had told me they had already dined with the kids), they even fed me with what they had left over from dinner! For six hours (until nearly three in the morning!), we shared stories and laughed the evening away. I learned wonderful things about their lives, including intersections with our family I hadn't known about. They even shared some encouraging stories about my kids, which made me think my kids might have actually been listening to me all this time.

The next day, encouraged by this modest initiative on my part, my wife baked chocolate chip cookies, and we walked "cookie deliveries" around to the new neighborhood friends. Given that I was headed out on a business trip the following day, I passed along some Boston Celtics tickets to the couple I'd spent time with the night before. They texted me a picture from the game later that evening. I was pleasantly surprised to see they'd invited a second couple from our neighborhood to join them.

I relearned an old principle that evening: you never know what experiences lie in your community, on your street, or even in the house next door. These opportunities may not happen as often as we'd like in our very busy lives. Sometimes we must choose to make them happen. But when another person—be it a friend, a neighbor, a stranger, or perhaps even a perceived adversary—intersects our path, we can still set down our devices and make time to talk.

You and I need people—we all need people. We can and will find that electricity between us when we acknowledge this fact, starting by engaging in person, one conversation at a time.

# CHAPTER 6

# YOU ARE NOT ALONE

## SHARE YOUR HIGHS AND LOWS

Behavioral psychologist B. F. Skinner believed that everything in life—science, child-rearing, drug addiction—is about control. Free will, he said, is an illusion. Dim the lights just right, spray the perfect perfume, give a well-timed treat, and you can make anyone do anything you want.

It's a creepy idea, but it made a big splash in the 1960s. In a world where the president could be killed by an unknown gunman, where the most powerful nation on earth could lose major battles to ragtag guerrilla fighters, and where young women were throwing their bras into bonfires in front of the White House, there was something oddly comforting to Skinner's message. Nothing is random. Nothing is unpredictable.

Soon enough, Skinner was famous for his "operant conditioning chambers," which were metal boxes he built himself. Every detail was finely tuned: the humidity, the noise level, the air pressure, the temperature. He put pigeons, rats, and, it is rumored, children in them and slowly, meticulously taught them to do things no one thought possible. His rats communicated about food and did tricks on demand. He claimed he could control when babies cried. During World War II, he even successfully demonstrated that his pigeons could guide ballistic missiles.

The US military didn't trust his pigeon soldiers, and rightfully so, but there was a reason his experiments were so successful. If you control every detail of a creature's environment, you can make them learn anything you want—as long as you change only one thing at a time.

Imagine you put four hundred healthy rats in four hundred identical chambers and gave them the exact same food at the exact same time in the exact same way, then turned the humidity up to 100 percent. If most of them lost their hair, stopped eating, or stopped exercising in their new muggy homes, you would know their state was most likely due to humidity. It was the only thing that changed. In other words, if you keep everything in the environment the same except for one factor, then all other factors in the environment are meaningless. Unless, of course, if the one factor you change alters the other factors in the environment in ways you didn't expect.

President Nixon's "war on drugs" treated America as one of Skinner's boxes. His administration looked at the statistics—skyrocketing drug-related homicides and hospitalizations—and treated everything as a symptom of only one problem: drug possession. The theory was that if we could take care of the drug problem, the other problems of society would follow suit.

But America isn't one of Skinner's boxes. By declaring a war on just one thing, Nixon created an environment that caused circumstances from which we still have not recovered. Nixon's war on drugs included greatly expanding the size and power of federal drug control agencies and pushing through mandatory sentencing and no-knock drug raids. The number of people incarcerated for drug offenses rose immediately, and this trend has continued for several decades, from 40,900 in 1980 to 452,964 in 2017.[1] Today more people are behind bars for a drug offense than the number of people who were in prison or jail for any crime in 1980. And according to the NAACP, while white Americans have been shown to buy and sell drugs at the same rate as African Americans, they are still only one-sixth as likely to be incarcerated.[2]

In the years since Nixon's war on drugs, we have tried to fix our mistakes by pointing at new villains—irresponsible doctors, dishonest pharmaceutical companies, or our country's own moral decline. And

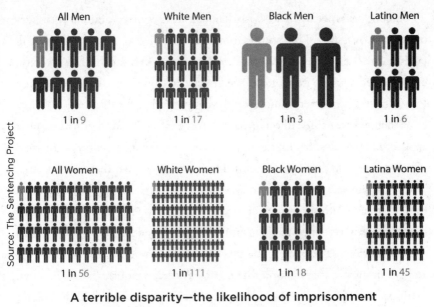

**A terrible disparity—the likelihood of imprisonment for black men in comparison with others.**

still, as Andrew Sullivan suggested in his essay "The Poison We Pick," "we miss a deeper American story."[3]

Throughout most of the twentieth century, there was a hot debate in the medical community over just how addictive opioids are. Pharmaceutical companies funded misleading research, many scientists drew sweeping conclusions based on tiny sample sizes, and it wasn't until researchers returned to their tried-and-true method—putting rats in boxes, à la B. F. Skinner—that the deeper issue became clear.

Each rat was put in its own box and given two water supplies: one clear, pure water, the other laced with morphine. The rats drank from the drugged water supply over and over again, neglecting the pure water, and food, until they faced their early deaths.

Those studies opened our eyes and served to silence some harmful misinformation. But still, something did not sit well with researcher Bruce Alexander.

Alexander lived in Canada around the time many soldiers returned from the Vietnam War, and it had slowly leaked to the public that around

20 percent of American and Canadian soldiers reported addiction to heroin while overseas. The home front was horrified to learn this. Rehab facilities stocked their inventory. Family members read pamphlets. Nixon even created a whole new office: the Special Action Office for Drug Abuse Prevention. Our society hunkered down, preparing for disaster.

Then, what seemed like a miracle: Jerome Jaffe, the addiction researcher appointed by Nixon to run the new office, found that *95 percent* of the men who became addicted in Vietnam did not relapse once they were home. While relapse rates of American civilians were often as high as 90 percent, these soldiers, without rehab centers, without gradually weaning off their supply, quietly returned to their families and started anew.[4]

How was this possible? The public rejected the data almost immediately. The newspapers claimed it must have been politically influenced or improperly gathered. Jaffe reported the office "spent months, if not years, trying to defend the integrity of the study."[5]

Forty years later, the results of that study *are* widely accepted, but the question remains: If addiction is such a powerful force, how were some people able to just snap out of it?

Alexander thought of those rats with their morphine bottles, refusing food and water until they died. He imagined himself in one of those metal boxes, isolated and bored. He thought that if the only escape from that box was a hit of morphine, he could easily overdose too.

All at once, he realized the great error of Skinner's boxes. Even if you keep everything in the environment the same, there is no way to magically erase it from the equation. In fact, environment, in its fullness, could be the main character in the story.

Instead of building metal boxes with endless knobs and controls, Alexander and his colleagues built a "rat park," about two hundred times the surface area of a typical laboratory cage. They included running tubes, food, and water. He filled the park with a couple of dozen male and female rats that were free to socialize, run around, have sex. The final touch? A standard water bottle next to an unending supply of sweetened morphine.

The individually caged rats drank the morphine solution nineteen times more frequently than the rats in the park. The park rats tried the morphine occasionally but actively avoided it most days. Rats raised in cages who later moved to the park were much more likely to drink the morphine solution than the rats raised in the park, but remarkably, they preferred the more diluted forms of the solution. Most notably, as soon as the morphine disrupted their social behavior, the addicted rats stopped drinking it, even while showing signs of withdrawal.[6]

Experiments like this have been repeated and reimagined for decades. A 2018 study published in *Nature Neuroscience* showed that rats given the choice between methamphetamine and/or heroin and socializing with other rats overwhelmingly chose to play rather than get high. This was true for rats exposed to drugs for the first time *and rats who had already become addicted.*[7]

It turns out that no distraction from drug use—not food, not exercise, not free space—is as powerful as simply giving the test subject another animal to play with.

More Americans died from drug overdoses last year than in the entire Vietnam War. And over two million are hooked on some form of opioid painkiller. This crisis, however, feels different from other drug crises in history. It doesn't camp out among marginalized groups and stay there. Rather, it is most rampant among middle-class white Americans. It hasn't accompanied a rise in crime or violence. In fact, it began with a drop in both. As Sam Quinones put it in his investigative book *Dreamland,* "Children of the most privileged group in the wealthiest country in the history of the world are getting hooked and dying in almost epidemic numbers from substances meant to, of all things, numb pain."[8]

Our next question should be: What pain are we trying to numb?

## The Loneliness Epidemic

When Alexis de Tocqueville visited America in 1830, he was astounded to find a culture of community. "Americans of all ages, conditions, and all dispositions" he wrote, "constantly unite together."[9] It was the secret ingredient to American exceptionalism—what made our democracy work. Up until recently, as much as we disagreed, our differences were tempered by doing life together: sharing meals, decorating the community center for a party, working on the PTA, or bringing food to church.

For many throughout the ages, one key contributor to having a "built-in community" has been marriage.* Today, however, fewer people are getting married than ever before, and fewer still are staying married. But the people putting off marriage aren't those you might expect.

We often hear about the decline of marriage and might assume it is the consequence of college-educated women prioritizing their careers, or unmarried millennial couples living together in sky-rises in New York City, but these demographics account for a very small portion of the drop in American marriage. Journalist Timothy Carney calls this the "Lena Dunham Fallacy," which means ascribing to cultural elites trends that actually started in the working class.[10]

In fact, in 2016 about 70 percent of college-educated women were married by age forty, while approximately half of women at that age without college degrees were married. In other words, while a decline in marriage is creeping across the board, working-class Americans are far less likely to be married or to have married friends or married parents.

Another key contributor to community over time has been religious affiliation. And perhaps the most pronounced change is in the so-called Bible Belt, which now looks a lot different than you might think. Peter Beinart's 2017 research found that "the percentage of white Republicans with no religious affiliation has nearly tripled since 1990."[11] And while the United States is still a religious nation overall—a recent Gallup poll said 72 percent of Americans report that religion is very important to

---

*    Generalizations of all kinds are always problematic when applied to individual cases. There are of course untold millions of people who live as "singles" and have great connection and community, while many who are married find themselves deeply isolated and lonely.

them—only 37 percent of Americans were found to attend church or synagogue weekly or almost weekly.

That demographic—reportedly religious but not part of a religious community—can tell us a lot. They report much higher rates of divorce and addiction than their churchgoing counterparts. They were even found to have lower life expectancies and a higher risk of suicide.

While all Americans must decide for themselves what role, if any, faith will play in their lives, undeniably, an element of community connection is lost when a church closes its doors.

Within our political parties, some of us are connected—some of us aren't. The Pew Research Center found that around four in ten Americans, regardless of political leaning or income bracket, expressed support for a candidate on social media. Working-class Americans, however, were far less likely to participate in political activity that involved physically attending an event, making friends, or speaking face-to-face. While 21 percent of citizens with postgraduate degrees attended a political event or rally in 2018, only 6 percent of citizens without a college degree attended a political event. And citizens without these degrees were also around half as likely to attend a local government meeting than their more educated peers.[12]

Have you ever watched an old black-and-white movie where the beautiful damsel gets her heart broken and falls gravely ill? Years ago, dying of a broken heart was a completely accepted plot twist. Turns out, it's not implausible. In fact, it goes a long way in describing what is happening to us at an alarming rate.

We have more access to medicine and health care in this century than any civilization has ever had, and yet the life expectancy of Americans has fallen for three of the past four years. That hasn't happened since World War I, when a worldwide flu pandemic—known as the Spanish flu, which we are all generally familiar with given coronavirus reporting—killed nearly seven hundred thousand Americans.

In the past twenty years, overdoses have quadrupled, and deaths due to opioids have increased sixfold. Suicide rates have grown by a third.

In fact, more young Americans die per year from suicide than car accidents.[13] The bottom line is that in America in the twenty-first century, we are literally dying of despair. Loneliness is now a medical condition. Dr. Julianne Holt-Lunstad, a professor of psychology and neuroscience at Brigham Young University, and Dr. Nancy Donovan, a psychiatrist who specializes in geriatrics and neurology at Boston's Brigham and Women's Hospital, analyzed over three hundred thousand people (nearly all were adults, and a substantial majority of them were middle-aged and older) and scored them in their indicators of community connection. They found that the people with low scores of perceived social connections carried a similar risk of early death to people who smoke fifteen cigarettes a day. Those with high scores of perceived connection were 50 percent less likely to die prematurely.[14]

Loneliness is also bad for the heart, and not just metaphorically. Dr. Redford B. Williams from Duke University found that lonely people are far more likely to develop heart disease and have heart attacks. Being chronically lonely carries about the same risks as being obese.

Loneliness is associated with an increased risk of disability,[15] coronary heart disease and stroke, high blood pressure, depression,[16] cognitive decline,[17] suicide in advanced age, and even clinical dementia.[18] One study showed it increases a person's chances of dying prematurely by up to 50 percent.[19] Other studies put the number as high as 60 percent.[20]

Think about the seriousness of that for one moment. Now, if I asked you to conjure up an antismoking ad in your head, most of you would be able to imagine some of the (often gruesome) images that have been used. And while these campaigns have attempted, for decades, to make smoking uncool, the even larger public health crisis—loneliness—has gone largely ignored.

To remedy that, Cigna, a global health services company, presented a large study in 2018 on loneliness. Some people, perhaps those who were not aware of the ever-growing data connecting loneliness and poor physical health, wondered why an insurance company would conduct such a study, assuming this topic would be better addressed by people like Dr. Phil.

However, the results of the Cigna survey were pretty dismal and indicated what some call a "loneliness epidemic."[21]

Writer Andrew Sullivan described it like this: "What has happened in the past few decades is an accelerated waning of all these traditional American supports for a meaningful, collective life, and their replacement with various forms of cheap distraction. Addiction—to work, to food, to phones, to TV, to video games, to porn, to news, and to drugs—is all around us."[22]

The great Mother Teresa said it best: "Loneliness is the leprosy of the modern world."[23]

## Doing Life Together

Rugged individualism captured the American imagination long before John Wayne rode off into the sunset in his many classic films. The idea of self-sustaining citizens is foundational to our nation, but I'm afraid we red-blooded Americans have taken it a bit too far.

Loneliness is a condition that sometimes embarrasses people more than if they had a physical disease. After all, diseases have names and antidotes. *Take two pills and call me in the morning.* But as Robert Putnam pointed out, sometimes the more important part of that oft-recited sentence is the last part. "Call me in the morning" indicates a certain level of connectivity that helps soothe what ails us.[24]

To stay connected at my house, we long practiced a dinner tradition. As we eat, we go around the table and allow each person to describe their "high" and "low" of the day. Sometimes a person might report all highs. Sometimes someone might report all lows. Usually, a combination of good and bad afflicts us all. With a family of six, there's almost always something going on.

At one point I noticed such a high level of "things that need attention" that I wondered whether we had a higher level of drama than others. To consider this question, I developed a formula—a family happiness index, if you will—that helps provide a proper expectation of "smooth sailing" when it comes to families.

Here's how it works.

First, focus on yourself. Figure the percentage of days in which you are generally doing well. Though this varies from person to person, it's pretty easy to determine your percentage. For me, I'm happy and content approximately 80 percent of my days. Others who are recovering from various traumas or emotional wounds might be happy less frequently. To help figure this out for yourself, jot down a plus or a minus in your journal at the end of the next ten days. You might find that you are happier than I am (nine or ten out of ten), are right in the middle (five out of ten), or tend toward the melancholy (by being happy four or fewer days out of ten).

Next, make this assessment of all the members of your family. Most of the time, you can just assign a pretty accurate percentage to others in your close orbit since you spend so much time considering and being affected by the happiness levels of your family members.

Now multiply the "happiness probability percentage" of one family member by the next, and the next, and the next.

I'll show you how this works by calculating the Kingston family happiness index. Though each member of my family has varying levels of happiness and contentedness, let's assume for the purposes of this thought experiment that each person's general happiness percentage is the same as mine. That means I'd multiply that 80 percent figure six times. I'll spare you the math, but here's what I've found.

With six human beings living with each other, the chances of every one of the Kingston family members doing well at the same time is only 26 percent, or approximately one out of every four days. And that's with a pretty optimistic view of each person's well-being.

What this little experiment shows us is probably what we already know too well, at least in our bones. Human beings have problems, and they pop up more frequently than you might expect.

---

In 1992 Admiral James Stockdale stood on the stage of the vice presidential debates as the running mate of independent candidate Ross Perot. His opening lines were not delivered with the political flair needed for the moment.

"Who am I? Why am I here?"

His intended rhetorical opening did not lead to a more substantial introduction and understanding of Stockdale. In fact, Americans across the nation wondered whether the relatively older candidate knew the answer to those questions.

It's a shame that this national hero, a former prisoner of war, was so mischaracterized by a few lines. Stockdale was a true American hero. Imprisoned in the Vietnamese "Hanoi Hilton," he spent four years in solitary confinement, two years in leg irons, and was denied food and medical care despite a broken bone in his back and a dislocated knee. He was also tortured over twenty times.[25] Yet he survived.

What was different between him and those who died in prison? The answer might surprise you. Stockdale explained that the people who didn't make it were optimists.

"They were the ones who said, 'We're going to be out by Christmas.' And Christmas would come, and Christmas would go. Then they'd say, 'We're going to be out by Easter.' And Easter would come, and Easter would go. And then Thanksgiving, and then it would be Christmas again. And they died of a broken heart."[26]

Though Stockdale believed he would one day get out, he was dedicated to thinking about the present moment. Author Jim Collins called this the "Stockdale Paradox," which he defined this way: "You must retain unwavering faith that you can and will prevail in the end, regardless of the difficulties, *AND* *at the same time* . . . confront the most brutal facts of your current reality, whatever they might be."[27]

Why am I talking about a former prisoner of war and failed political candidate? You can forgive me for having a soft spot in my heart for non-politicians who don't quite master the dark arts of politics. But mainly, I think his observation about clear thinking is critical to understanding the amount of "regular pain" we feel in our lives.

I hope you have not experienced torture in a foreign land. But many of us have an unhealthy perspective of our current reality. So many live with the social media–influenced notion that some families have it all together—not only is everyone doing fine, they are doing fine while wearing great clothing, perfect makeup, and permanently styled hair. Because we're inundated with constant messages from society that everyone else is doing oh–so–well, it's easy to get discouraged by life's challenges. However, the family happiness index does a better job than Instagram at illustrating what actually goes on behind the filtered lenses.

Here's what's often being obscured in the modern era: life is just hard. We need to have faith that we can survive our current ordeals while at the same time dealing with the realities we're given. Plus, we have to recognize what we're up against before we can admit we need each other.

I fear I lost you at the phrase "need each other." Some of you, those who pride yourself on your self-sufficiency and perhaps even congratulate yourself on your loner tendencies, recoil at the very thought. But the fact of the matter is that we all need each other to survive.

For example, right now I'm typing on a iPad that other people made somewhere across the globe. I wear clothing that someone made on a machine. I wear shoes that someone fashioned. I eat food that someone else invariably grew and harvested. I listen to music that someone else performed, recorded, and made available to me through iTunes. I pay for my purchases through technology I can't begin to fathom. I even live in a house that other people built.

Whether or not we like to admit it, our physical survival and enjoyment of life depend on a multitude of strangers we'll never meet. And our immediate community can have an even deeper impact than these far-flung connections.

## I Need You

Let me provide you with a description of an aspect of my life that I feel I have gotten right. From an early age, I have promoted the value of being together. To that end, when we moved to Boston, I convened a guys' group, while my wife, Jean, met with a group of their wives.

I gathered these particular men because my path crossed with each of them in various ways. Some I met through church, which is usually a good way to connect with people on a deeper level. No matter the circumstances of your life, you can find people with whom to do life: people everywhere long for true connections with other human beings. The only requirement is the humility to admit that we need each other.

Yes, humility. People who choose to be in close community with one another must reach out and say, "I want to be a part of your life." That's not easy. The next step is to figure out the structure that allows connection between each other's lives in a meaningful way.

Matthew Lieberman reminds us, "We all need people to love and respect, and we all need people who love and respect us. We do not always recognize these needs, and we may not see them influencing those around us, but they are still there nonetheless."[28]

## Shared Burdens, Shared Joys

An old proverb informs this desire to be together with friends: a shared burden is half a burden, a shared joy is double joy.

Once a dear friend of mine considered running for Congress. As he considered this move, I helped his wife prepare for the inevitable public intrusion into their family. One evening while we were discussing the pros and cons of the potential campaign, I conducted an informal "vetting process" for her. That term originated from veterinarians who would check on racehorses' health to make sure they could last a whole race. In politics, it is the unpleasant process of describing anything in one's past that could come out and embarrass a candidate during a political race.

I remember sitting at a table in the beautiful mountain lodge as we began the process. When I asked her if she had any former boyfriends who might come out of the woodwork, she hesitantly told me about a string of bad relationship experiences. Eventually, she told me the original source of the pain: she had been the victim of a pedophile at a young age.

As we sat among the stunning mountains, wide-open skies, and endless views, I ached as I listened. I offered advice on some of the political ramifications of her past and suggested a counselor might help her sort through these issues. What could I possibly offer in terms of practical advice? Later she told me that our conversation began a search for healing that led to her finally facing down the demons that had haunted her during her entire adult life. I didn't offer tidy counsel because I didn't have any magic words that could take away the pain. However, there was something powerful about taking the secret out of its hiding place that robbed it of its control over her.

A Bible verse reminds us that "everything exposed by the light becomes visible."[29] Doing life with others is effectively shedding a light on our lives so that the good is illuminated and the shadows grow dim.

## It's Simple but Not Easy

My group of guys has met together for over twenty years. Over the course of that time, "doing life together" meant we'd pour ourselves into one another's lives by asking what was going on in their lives and what they were wrestling with.

Sometimes they shared the happy news of success: when they or their children did something well, when they were on a hot streak with their jobs, or a transaction had gone well, or their relationships with their wives were going really well. But more often than not, burdens were shared too.

We dealt with eating too much, drinking too much, and indulging in pornography. Some of us, at various times, had anger issues or battled sadness. I knew what went on with my friends' children, some of whom were deeply troubled (along with my own, at times). I knew my friends made bad decisions at work that threatened their very livelihood. Some were laid off, others fired. Still others struggled to uphold their marriage vows, and some faced divorce. Remarkably, our son who returned from his wilderness therapy experience moved in with one of the group members for a portion of every week. We did this because we thought our son would do better with the discipline of living outside our home some of the time. Of course, we could do this only because these friends are willing to share our burdens, which is an extraordinary gift.

Perhaps these sound like normal issues that plague everyone, but if you put a group of people together, new and unique complications can arise that will surprise you.

One day one of our members (we will call him James) announced that his wife (we will call her Jessica) was diagnosed with terminal cancer. Jean and I were committed to and loved James and Jessica and their family, with whom we had spent so much time over the decades.

As we collectively tried to bear the weight of such a grave situation, we knew this wasn't going to be a small investment of time or emotion. We knew we'd watch as Jessica slowly climbed down into the grave, and we'd have to climb down into that hole with James as he grieved. Slowly, ever so slowly, we knew he'd come up for air. But this process would not stop after the funeral, or perhaps even years after the funeral. We were going to be in this for a long time, and it was going to be excruciating.

And there was another complicating factor. While Jessica and I did some remarkable things together (she was an outstanding project manager, and she threw her great capacity into some partnerships around the city that we worked on together), we didn't always get along. We all have our relationship issues, and we don't always know the source, whether it's you or the other person or both. While she was an important member of the wives' group—and our groups intersected a lot—it became obvious that she and I were not destined to be the closest of friends.

I was away when I received word that she'd died. Here's a confession I regret having to share: I was afraid of coming back for the funeral. I didn't—and still don't—entirely know why. Maybe I don't handle death well in certain circumstances. Maybe I didn't know how I'd handle her being eulogized. Maybe I would feel guilty about something from my past with her. Whatever it was, I knew I had to get over myself. It wasn't about me. It was about being present. I knew I didn't have to do anything other than show up. Presence is a gift. And in a strange way, perhaps it was made even more valuable by the underlying complexities of our imperfect relationship.

When I walked into the church on that very sad day, James knew I had his back. While I was there for him, the circumstances helped shape me too. I saw that my fears were misdirected, even selfish. I was reminded that it's always important to show up, in person, for the big events in life and death.*

———————

Over the course of two decades, people have come in and out of our group. Some guys didn't click with the group. Some, for whatever reason, didn't fit easily into the group, didn't get the dynamic, or dominated the conversation. Some weren't relationally reciprocal. Others weren't willing to accept criticism.

In fact, one of the most dramatic conversations I've ever had in my life happened on my front porch with one of the members of this group. Another group member and I were gently confronting this guy about his decision to commute to New York from Boston for work. "We see the path you're going down, and we sense it's not going to give you the peace and purpose you want." The truth was that given his substance abuse history, we feared that the choices he might make in all that time alone would hurt him, his marriage, and his family. Though we expressed our concerns with as much delicacy and kindness as we could muster, he didn't take it well.

He accused us of ganging up on him, stormed off the porch, and quit the group. I carry tremendous pain to this day knowing that he did end up losing his family, wife, and health. Our relationship has never been the same, although I continue to hope and pray for its eventual renewal.

It was a hard moment for the group, one of those unexpected moments of friction that would threaten the cohesion of any group. But

---

\* I of course met with James to review this portion (as I have met with many whose stories I have shared throughout the book), particularly given he had no prior knowledge of my feelings about the funeral. The time we spent meeting and discussing our lives together, remembering both the good and painful times throughout, was itself a great gift.

you have to be willing to have hard conversations and make adjustments. And together, as a group, we survived.

Your friends are worth it. In some form or fashion, every single person needs this sort of community in their life. There are no rules—just do it. And if at first you don't succeed, try and try again.

Consciously live your life with a group of people.

It's simple, but it's never easy.

In this digitally driven world we live in, the likelihood of being mistaken, misunderstood, or mischaracterized is *real*. Life is complicated and seems downright cruel at times. Friends make it more bearable on bad days, more beautiful on good days.

In his book *The Tech-Wise Family*, my old friend Andy Crouch (with whom I participated in a similar group in the Boston area in the 1990s) wrote that early in his marriage, he and his wife made a pact. At least one of them would try to attend every single wedding they were invited to and every single funeral. "We show up in person for the big events of life," he wrote. "We learn how to be human by being fully present at our moments of greatest vulnerability."[30]

Although life is invariably complex and we never achieve the goal of being at all the important events to our satisfaction (you can't be in more than one place at one time and have to prioritize), my wife, Jean, and I made a similar commitment. Very recently, a beloved sister-in-law underwent a major surgery in another city, and we mutually agreed that Jean should go to be with the family for the important surgery day as well as the days that followed, while I would stay behind to oversee the home front and family. Her brother declined the offer, undoubtedly trying to be respectful of Jean's time, confident that all would be well and that he had things in order. Jean and I agreed that, notwithstanding his feedback, this was too important and wasn't something they should endure alone. To their surprise, Jean walked into the hospital room in advance of the surgery and remained for a couple of days.

I know that they were encouraged and happy to have her there. For Jean, her time or the outcome was not the priority. What mattered most for Jean, and what was most uplifting for her brother and his family, was her sitting next to them in the waiting room and praying with them beside our sister-in-law's hospital bed.

———

If some of our leading social figures were one of those researchers examining the cages full of rats, they might stroll down the aisles at night, clipboard in hand, measuring the morphine solutions and wondering why these rats were dying at such an alarming rate. They might try to invent new medicine that alleviates pain without leaving the rubble of dependence in its wake. Or if that didn't work, they might be tempted to try a political solution like eliminating access to the drug altogether, even if it would keep millions of people in chronic pain without comfort. In their concern for these creatures, their ideas might have been complicated and frantic, jumping from problem to problem, leading to questions that only led to more questions.

But the researchers knew what to do. They simply gave the rats some friends.

Though we need to rewrite outdated policies and invest everything we can in medical research, not all of us are speaking on the Senate floor or poring over data sheets at Harvard Medical School. Nor should we. Instead, we have the much greater task: to fight the epidemic of loneliness and, person by person, brick by brick, build communities that can do life together.

And they will need constant rebuilding.

Andrew Sullivan suggested, "One way of thinking of postindustrial America is to imagine it as a former rat park, slowly converting into a rat cage."[31]

The solution to loneliness won't come from our leaders and their policies. It will come from the people—you and me—actively, collectively choosing a life together rather than apart.

PART 2

WHO
WE
ARE

# CHAPTER 7

# WE ARE MORE ALIKE
# THAN DIFFERENT

## RESPOND INSTEAD OF REACT

A recent *Saturday Night Live* episode featured a game show skit called "Can I Play That?"[1] The rules seemed simple enough, as host Denny Glans (played by Kenan Thompson) explained. He would describe a role in an upcoming movie, and the three "working actors," David, Jackie, and Lawrence (played by Idris Elba, Cecily Strong, and Beck Bennett), would buzz in from their podiums to answer yes or no. But given this was *SNL*, the game was filled with traps, poking fun at the complex interpersonal maze of perceptions and reactions we find ourselves in today.

After explaining the rules, host Glans gave the contestants a warm-up question.

**Glans:** "For example, it was just announced that Will Smith will play the father of the Williams sisters. But can he play that?"

Beck Bennett's character, Lawrence, pops his buzzer excitedly.

**Glans:** "Lawrence?"

**Lawrence:** "Yes, of course. He'll do a great job."

A sharp buzzer is heard, indicating Lawrence is wrong.

**Glans:** "Ooohhh, anybody else?"

Cecily Strong's character, Jackie, buzzes in confidently.

**Jackie:** "He absolutely cannot. He's not black enough."

Idris Elba's character, David, cuts a glance at Jackie.

**David [brows furrowed]:** "What?"

**Glans [pointing affirmatively]:** "You are right, Jackie."

**David [brows still furrowed]:** "Wait, wait, wait. Is this real?"

**Glans [grinning]:** "It sure is, because this game is produced by Twitter. One mistake will kill you."

The audience laughed as the Twitter logo appeared on-screen. The game continued with questions about whether the actors could play the roles of a blind person, a secretly-Mexican astronaut, Caitlyn Jenner, a half-Asian person, and Michael Jackson's ghost. One by one, the actors were scolded for thinking they could play the role or rewarded for indicating they clearly couldn't—unless the actor was Rami Malek, who was somehow magically allowed to play anyone.

The game finished with a lightning round where the contestants had ten seconds to list as many roles as they could that they'd be allowed to play. Beck Bennett's character, Lawrence (a middle-aged white man who finally understands the rules), went first and answered, "White guy . . . white guy who gained fifty pounds . . . white guy who is a slave owner," which is rewarded with a *ding-ding-ding-ding* for a perfect answer.[2]

Regardless of whether you fall in any of the "people categories" *SNL* described, or however you might identify yourself, you wouldn't be alone if you feel unsettled by what seems to be an ever-changing rule book of social etiquette. Katherine Timpf recalled some of the extreme political correctness she's covered during her time as a journalist:[3]

- Colorado State University asks students to avoid gendered emojis to be more inclusive on social media.
- Skinny eyebrows are declared cultural appropriation.
- A lawmaker claims a General Joseph Hooker sign is offensive to women.

- "God bless you" is declared an anti-Islamic microaggression.
- A professor proclaims small chairs in preschools are sexist, problematic, and disempowering.[4]
- The size of chairs in general is deemed a microaggression against overweight people.

There's no question we've been insensitive—often much worse—to many of our citizens over the course of our history. And there's no question we can never lose our commitment to compassionately pursue a "more perfect union." This *must* always remain in focus, and in some respects, we're making strides. But are we simultaneously losing our grip on the reality that we have far more in common than not?

It's easy to feel lost in this world of differences. The country feels more divided by the minute. But if you step back from the intensity of the moment and look at the context of history, you will find that divisions are entirely normal human nature. Jonah Goldberg described this phenomenon in his book *Suicide of the West*:

> Given time and incentives, any group of humans will start to see themselves as a cohesive group, a caste or aristocratic class. Just as any random group of dogs—strays and purebreds alike—will, if put together, quickly form a pack with a collective identity, humans will do the same thing given time and the right inducements. The children in *Lord of the Flies*, contestants on *Survivor*, college students in the Stanford prison experiments, members of the Seattle Seahawks, police, firemen, marines, Copts, Sunnis, teachers' unions, street gangs, college professors—the list is as endless as the subdivision of labor and identity in any society.[5]

As Goldberg went on to observe, this natural human tendency to divide ourselves into groups is neither good nor bad; it is simply a fact. So the issue is not new, and it isn't even "wrong." Against the backdrop of human nature, and with the ideals of who we are as Americans (a topic we will discuss further in subsequent chapters), our task is to find the most fitting degree of unity together, with the understanding that we will always be to some extent divided.

Unfortunately, in the modern world we live in, the task is made all the more challenging given the many forces at work to intentionally lie to us and amplify differences between these "people categories" in destructive ways. In chapter 5 we discussed the challenges of the relatively new and amazing technologies that keep us connected round-the-clock and round-the-planet. We've now stumbled onto one more—we haven't yet figured out how to respond instead of react in a modern age where falsehoods are disseminated like digital wildfire. Recall that in the digital world, things are often false to some degree (even if there is no intention to lie). And unfortunately, some malicious people often *intentionally* peddle lies in an effort to exploit differences.

The list of intentional efforts to tell false stories is nearly limitless, but the following are some examples:

- An intentionally doctored video of a prominent American political figure was widely circulated. The video, which was slowed in tailored sections so that the politician appeared to be drunkenly slurring her words, was seen many millions of times, with substantial numbers of viewers not recognizing it had been faked.[6]
- "Disinformation is increasingly based on images as opposed to text," said Paul Barrett.[7] As a consequence, Instagram could become a new platform for spreading disinformation, as news falsifiers rely on images and proxy accounts to create and circulate fake content.
- Facebook estimates that up to 5 percent of all accounts are now fake, a percentage that is increasing, even as the company deleted 2.2 *billion* fake accounts in recent months.[8]
- A Pew Research Center survey last year found that two-thirds of tweeted links to popular websites came from nonhuman users (bots or other automated accounts).[9]

So if you're tired of trying to decipher truth from untruth and accuracy from inaccuracy, it is because there is a near-constant effort to make you believe things that are false. And far more likely than not, the falsehoods are designed to make you think ill of people who aren't in "your" group, and instead are in another "people category" perceived to be in conflict with yours.

As a consequence, we are all exhausted. This is precisely the point of this modern form of misinformation. Garry Kasparov, arguably the greatest chess player in history and survivor of some very dark days in Russia (so an astute observer of the use of propaganda), has observed, "The point of modern propaganda isn't only to misinform or push an agenda. It is to exhaust your critical thinking, to annihilate truth."[10] Peter Pomerantsev, author of *This Is Not Propaganda*, said, "They spread the sense that . . . the truth is unknowable, and all that's left in this confusing world is me."[11]

One of the great social observers of the twentieth century, Hannah Arendt, observed this dynamic in an age when disinformation spread much more slowly, by hand-delivered newsprint and similar means: "The result of a consistent and total substitution of lie for factual truth is not that the lie will now be accepted as truth and truth be defamed as a lie, but that the sense by which we take our bearings in the real world—and the category of truth versus falsehood is among the means to this end—is being destroyed."[12]

As a consequence, the sheer volume of assaults on fact and truth is undermining us not just in politics and government but in business, technology, science, and health care as well.[13] Today a majority of Americans say they've lost trust in the federal government and one another, according to a Pew Research Center survey.[14] And in another recent survey, fully 55 percent of Democrats believe that Republicans are dangerous to the country, while 58 percent of Republicans believe the same about Democrats.[15]

What is the net effect of all this? The *New Yorker* interviewed General James Mattis in early 2017 while he was in the confirmation process to serve as the US Secretary of Defense. He was asked what worried him most in that new role. One might reasonably expect that given Mattis's responsibility to defend our nation, he would name an external threat, such as a nuclear North Korea, an emboldened Russia, or the threat of jihadist terrorism. Mattis's response was surprising, as he observed our principal threat to be "the lack of political unity in America. The lack of a fundamental friendliness. . . . If you lose any sense of being part of something bigger, then why should you care about your fellow-man?"[16]

I feel exhausted just writing about this. I suspect you feel the same way reading it! Living every day in the misinformed mess that divides us is wearing us all out. As a result, it's easy to get discouraged about the state of our world.

But what if we are actually more "together" than we think we are?

A group called More in Common published a recent study on this very subject. In it, they found that despite the binary opposition portrayed in the national conversation and catastrophized through misinformation campaigns, most of us—65 percent—want to find a mutually agreeable place so that together we can make positive progress. The study went on to observe the following:

> Political polls and years of knife-edge elections have convinced many that . . . [we are] trapped in a spiral of conflict and division. Our research uncovered a different story. . . . In talking to everyday Americans, we have found a large segment of the population whose voices are rarely heard above the shouts of the partisan tribes. These are people who believe that Americans have more in common than that which divides them. While they differ on important issues, they feel exhausted by the division in the United States. They believe that compromise is necessary in politics, as in other parts of life, and want to see the country come together and solve its problems.[17]

Even among those at the complete opposite ends of the political spectrum on major issues, a little over half (51 percent) still believe that "the people I agree with politically need to be willing to listen to others and compromise."[18]

Here is some hope: we've been in divided places before, and we know our way out. We just have to get back to the anchoring principle that what divides us is not greater than what unites us.

Nearly three decades ago, I started a fantasy baseball league. You probably know some fantasy league participants in one sport or another, but in the old-school fantasy league world before mainstream internet or email use, sports geeks like me had to really pay our dues. Once upon a time, we had to calculate our own results by checking newspapers and then use the US mail to send hard copies of our self-calculated results to our league commissioner. While I did this for years, as I recall it today, I can scarcely believe how hard we worked to make sports statistics fun before the dawn of the internet.

The greatest number of participants in my league were friends and acquaintances from Harvard Law School, where I attended at the time. Some were even older friends from my undergrad days. As time went on, friends from other avenues of life joined us, as did some friends of friends in the league. After some expansion and contraction through the years, the number of participants has firmed up at just under twenty guys. The group is diverse geographically (league members live from coast to coast, in the Northeast, mid-Atlantic, Southeast, South, Mountain West, and West Coast regions), equally diverse religiously (Christian, Jewish, atheist, agnostic) and politically (very conservative to very liberal), and also racially and ethnically diverse.

While we get together in person once annually for our auction/draft, and from time to time as we travel around the country (at the time of this writing one league member is flying in from the Bay Area to Boston for business and will stay with our family), the most unusual aspect of relationships in our league is our ongoing connection through email.

**Once upon a time, the draft weekend sports activities were football, basketball, or the armed forces fitness test (we used to tongue-in-cheek call it the "manly challenge")—by the time of this draft in Salt Lake City in 2019, curling was as far as we could go in our "manly challenge" pursuits!**

Because the people in the group are very opinionated and *really* enjoy sharing their views (and some are authors and professional writers), there have been hundreds of thousands of emails written on nearly every topic imaginable. We have discussed everything from sports to faith to politics to public policy to raising children to grieving lost family and friends.

And, oh, how we fight about issues that matter to us. Most often these arguments are constructive, but not always.

As a consequence, the relationships have grown strong, even across distance and racial, ethnic, political, and faith lines. Over time we have come to appreciate that whatever our differences, we are in this together.

Even still, as with all human relationships, our resolve gets tested from time to time.

During the summer of 2019, two league members were discussing a possible player addition. One member (we will call him Jim) is Caucasian, and the other (we will call Dan) is Chinese American.

Dan proposed a transaction involving Jordan Yamamoto, a Miami Marlins pitcher born in Hawaii; the last name Yamamoto traces back to the family's Japanese heritage. In an effort to be playful and amusing, Jim replied that he would approve only if all future reference to Mr. Yamamoto be as "Tojo." For those who don't know (I didn't!), Tojo Yamamoto was the ring name of Harold Watanabe, a Japanese American professional wrestler during World War II who caricatured Japanese dictator Hideki Tojo inside the ring.

This response triggered a temporarily heated exchange about race and cultural history. Dan explained that the shameful example of Tojo Yamamoto, who was asked to perform in a demeaning way to play to the prevailing stereotypes of his day (an American wrestler forced to play a hated enemy figure), illustrated the painful and racist experience of Asian Americans in the twentieth century. Jim clarified that for him, the wrestler's persona was no different from any comic book character; it was a neutral reference with no intended ethnic significance and a connection that didn't extend beyond a shared last name. Perhaps he and Dan just have different perspectives, Jim concluded.

While I obviously don't have full insight into what my friends were feeling, I sense it was something like the following. Jim felt confused and defensive. He had not intended to offend Dan. He had just made a joke. Why did Dan react this way? Why was he so sensitive? Dan, on the other hand, felt frustrated and hurt. Sure, perhaps Jim's intention wasn't to be offensive, but even then, how could he not be more aware of historical realities? That people of color had to accept cultural stereotypes that white culture dictated seemed so clear to him—why wasn't it clear to Jim?

In that moment, my two friends were faced with a decision. They could either react to their frustration, confusion, and pain or, in light of their shared history and experience together, respond with patience and a desire to understand each other.

Dan told Jim, "We're good," and proceeded to explain the cultural history around Tojo Yamamoto. He further explained that Jim's take of "different perspectives" is what makes race so loaded because what may be seen as a "neutral" reference (one made with neutral intention) is not actually neutral in the historical reality and lived experience of minority communities.

Dan explained. Jim listened. Together, they learned.

My friend Dan shared this exchange with me later that day, starting with his customary humor and finishing with an important insight: "If achieving fantasy league dominance means I have to engage in some racial reconciliation work, I will do so. This is an interesting window into why American hope . . . depends on 'small communities' like this fantasy baseball league, where people are willing to practice honesty and friendship."

There is nothing new under the sun, and those things that threaten to sever the relationships that connect us—disagreement, misunderstanding, ignorance, bitterness, contempt—have been around forever. But so have the principles that light the path forward, which is a path back together.

In one of the bestselling books of all time, a wonderful synthesis of all sorts of great thinkers before him, Stephen Covey explained it this way: "If I were to summarize in one sentence the single most important principle I have learned in the field of interpersonal relations, it would be this: Seek first to understand, then to be understood."[19]

Yes! The clearly distilled wisdom of the ages! As many will recognize, Covey's statement echoes Saint Francis's famous prayer.

> *O divine Master, grant that I may not so much seek*
> *to be consoled as to console,*
> *to be understood as to understand,*
> *to be loved as to love.*[20]

Even though we all know this is probably the right answer, being asked to do it in the heat of a moment when you feel misunderstood yourself is like being asked to eat your kale salad as a kid. Who wants to do that?

Jonathan Haidt, an NYU professor of psychology who wrote a classic about getting beyond our misunderstandings on the toughest topics, offered this insight:

> So the next time you find yourself seated beside someone from another
> matrix, give it a try. Don't just jump right in. Don't bring up morality
> until you've found a few points of commonality or in some other way
> established a bit of trust. And when you do bring up issues of morality,
> try to start with some praise, or with a sincere expression of interest.
> We're all stuck here for a while, so let's try to work it out.*[21]

Maybe there is a hint here—from my fantasy baseball league to Haidt—for all of us. Undoubtedly, when we start with some measure of common ground, we are more willing to look beyond our disagreements and misunderstandings.

Nevertheless, we will still disagree. We won't see eye-to-eye. And we may not even have clear common ground. What happens when the feelings get really heated—deep down heated—like anger, or worse?

Anger is one of the three poisons in the ancient religion of Buddhism; greed and ignorance are the other two, which, when you consider the primary reasons humans argue, seems pretty insightful. Together these three poisons are known as the cause of the cycle of *samsara* and rebirth whereby one has to make right one's wrongs in the previous life. Regarding anger specifically, Buddhism leaves no room for what would be called "righteous" or "justifiable" anger. All anger is seen as an impediment to the realization of one's life purpose.

While there is undoubtedly a lot to be said for these insights, in my view (and the view of many other psychological and religious traditions), the real poison lies not in anger itself but in something best described as contempt or bitterness. For human beings, generally, anger is a normal and completely understandable emotional reaction given particular personal

---

★    Haidt's "matrix" is what we are describing as a "people category."

and situational contexts. But what happens when that anger persists? When we hold on to anger, it festers and devolves into something more sinister, and we allow our hearts to become hardened toward others.

That is what we call contempt, or bitterness.

Nineteenth-century philosopher Arthur Schopenhauer defined contempt as "the unsullied conviction of the worthlessness of another."[22] Contempt, unlike anger, completely alters the way you see people. Rather than an emotion, it is a perspective so entrenched that it dehumanizes those who may not share your ideas and beliefs, leaving no space for understanding.

That is the observation made in *Love Your Enemies*, the latest book by Arthur C. Brooks, a premier American social scientist and longtime friend. In a speech given at Harvard University's Kennedy School, Brooks observed how this culture of contempt has seeped into our current politics: "We don't have an anger problem in American politics. We have a contempt problem. . . . If you listen to how people talk to each other in political life today, you notice it is with pure contempt."[23]

In distinguishing between anger and contempt, Brooks described anger as the (sometimes fierce) reaction to something you care about and that ultimately desires to bring back the other into the fold. Contempt, on the other hand, mocks, shames, belittles, and humiliates with the desire to exile completely. Contempt says, "You disgust me. You are beneath caring about."[24]

While contempt and bitterness are undeniably problems across our culture and country, they aren't felt only against other people categories. It may be fitting to look closer to home—literally, as close as you can get.

Dr. John Gottman, one of the world's foremost marriage researchers and cofounder of The Gottman Institute, identified contempt as the number one predictor of divorce. In his book *Why Marriages Succeed or Fail*, Gottman noted, "When contempt begins to overwhelm your relationship you tend to forget entirely your partner's positive qualities. . . . You can't remember a single positive quality or act. This immediate decay of admiration is an important reason why contempt ought to be banned from marital interactions."[25]

So it appears that contempt can destroy the connection of even the closest of relationships. In a recent *Atlantic* article about our culture of contempt and the groups whose mission it is to help melt away that iciness, Andrew Ferguson observed that techniques borrowed from marriage counseling and couples therapy may help us bridge the bitter divide between liberals and conservatives. He wrote, "Eliminating contempt may not be sufficient to save a relationship, but, as marriage research suggests, it is almost certainly necessary. Perhaps the same is true for the nation."[26]

It's not difficult these days to feel tempted to find a target for our anger. It's the right or the left or the rich or the poor or the white people or the black people. The truth is that people of every sort do infuriating things on a regular basis. That includes you and me. It is impossible to avoid some causes for anger, but letting that anger devolve into contempt, as the old saying goes, is like drinking poison and expecting the other person to suffer from it. There seems to be a lot of that suffering going around.

Consider the recent example of Ellen DeGeneres and Portia de Rossi, who were watching a football game with former president George W. Bush and his wife, Laura. They were shown on television laughing and enjoying each other's company. Many were outraged that "a gay Hollywood liberal," as Ellen described herself, would ever associate with—let alone laugh alongside—"a conservative Republican president."[27] Ellen subsequently told her viewers, "Here's the thing: I'm friends with George Bush. In fact, I'm friends with a lot of people who don't share the same beliefs that I have. We're all different, and I think that we've forgotten that it's okay that we're all different. When I say be kind to one another, I don't mean only the people that think the same way that you do. I mean be kind to everyone."[28]

The response infuriated many who used their social media accounts and magazine columns to express their anger. A writer named Naomi LaChance insisted, "You literally cannot be kind to everyone. You have to choose a side! Ellen certainly has."[29]

© Pablo Martinez Monsivais/AP/Shutterstock

**First Lady Michelle Obama hugs former president George W. Bush at the opening of the National Museum of African American History and Culture in September 2016.**

Michelle Obama rose to Ellen's defense. It is no secret that Obama's views are on the other end of the political spectrum from those of former president Bush, and they have different ideas about which policies are best for our country. But in an interview with *TODAY*'s Jenna Bush Hager (George W.'s daughter), Michelle spoke with a warmth and clarity on her and Bush's similarities and differences: "I had the opportunity to sit by your father at funerals, the highs and the lows, and we shared stories about our kids and our parents. Our values are the same. We disagree on policy, but we don't disagree on humanity. We don't disagree about love and compassion. I think that's true for all of us. It's just that we get lost in our fear of what's different."[30]

In 1998, University of Washington researchers Anthony Greenwald, Debbie McGhee, and Jordan Schwartz introduced the Implicit Association Test (IAT) through a series of three experiments that were designed to test the implicit (or unconscious) bias their subjects had to certain gender- and ethnic-related topics.[31] The purpose of the IAT is to measure, down to milliseconds, how long it takes a person to associate pairs of ideas. The premise of the test is simple: you'll be quicker at pairing concepts you already unconsciously associate with each other. You'll be slower at pairing concepts that you don't yet associate with each other. Such distinctions indicate what the researchers describe as "implicit attitudes" that "are manifest as actions or judgments that are under the control of automatically activated evaluation, without the performer's awareness of that causation."[32] For those of us who don't speak science, this means the unconscious associations our minds have already made, or not made, can form unconscious or unintentional stereotypes about the people around us. While the ultimate significance of the IAT continues to be a hotly debated topic in academic social science circles, the important observation it makes—and punctuates for us—is that our views may be more nuanced and deeply embedded than we believe them to be. They are not, however, completely outside our control.

In his influential book *Blink*, Malcolm Gladwell wrote about taking the IAT himself, one focused on race. As a man who is half black, imagine his horror when he learned that he had an unconscious pro-white bias.

I took the test a second time, and then a third time, and then a fourth time. . . . It made no difference. It turns out that more than 80 percent of all those who have ever taken the test end up having pro-white associations, meaning that it takes them measurably longer to complete answers when they are required to put good words into the "Black" category than when they are required to link bad things with black people. I didn't do quite so badly. On the Race IAT, I was rated as having a "moderate automatic preference for whites." But then again, I'm half black.[33]

Gladwell then asked what this meant. Was he a racist or a self-hating black person? What it meant is that two layers of associations can influence our views on others. First, there's the unconscious layer that is "implicit," as the IAT researchers call it. As you may recall from some long-ago class in psychology, famous psychologist Sigmund Freud labeled this unconscious layer as the "subconscious." The "implicit" layer doesn't involve any choice on our part and is based on our mind's aggregate conclusions of all the data we have absorbed over our entire life. This includes what our parents taught us; our experiences with people; the lessons we've taken from those interactions; the articles, blogs, and posts we've read; films, books, and videos we've taken in; and so on.* All this intake is constantly harmonized together into conclusions to, ultimately, help us survive by preparing our bodies to react to predetermined threats in an instant. It's extremely helpful in the context of an oncoming bus or a one-hundred-miles-an-hour foul ball at a baseball game. But it doesn't help us thoughtfully respond to other people.

But, thankfully, our unconscious layer is not the only layer that informs our thoughts about others. There's also the layer we consciously choose and willfully manifest through our actions. Since taking the IAT and learning of his implicit bias, Gladwell admitted the experience has taught him to consciously disregard his first impressions and spend more time getting to know people.

This is the cornerstone of our solution, our way out from this challenging moment. When we take the time to get to know one another, what is true statistically can become true experientially—we are more alike than different.

---

\*    What this tells us, at the very least: (1) what we feed our minds does in fact matter, and (2) the culture we live in, which feeds our minds both subtle and raw messages all day long, has a lot more influence than we might like to admit.

In America today:

We feel angry.

We feel hurt.

We feel unseen and misunderstood.

We feel saddened and despondent.

We feel deeply divided and separate.

These feelings come from very deep spaces, and none of our initial reactions are irrational or unreasonable. They are formed by our own version of the aggregate cultural and personal input that could prompt Gladwell to react to black people differently than white people. But as with Gladwell's decision to override his first impressions, what we do with our own implicit instincts is what matters. In short, do we indulge our instincts to:

Allow anger to harden into contempt?

Remain in our positions, inflexible?

Stay aloof and disconnected?

Tune out of relationships and the conversation, completely dispirited?

On the first page of her insightful book, *Looking Up*, Michele Sullivan, a woman born with dwarfism who has experienced a lifetime facing the implicit bias of others, made a key point about how we think about our initial reactions and how to overcome them: "Even if we know the swift conclusions we form are arbitrary, and many have been proven wrong before, we still carry a powerful, natural affection for the instincts we're counting on to survive in the world. We have to learn to override this instinct by remembering that surviving isn't the point of life. Thriving is. This requires embracing a broader perspective on others than the snap judgments our brains form at first glance."[34]

Sullivan's mom gave her advice as a young girl that she credits as the most important she ever received. "Always make the first move," her mom told her, so that others could quickly overcome the instant and largely unconscious conclusions formed from seeing her very small stature. "When other people get to know you," her mom continued, "they will no longer see you as being different."

So true! The more you take the initiative to get to know someone, the more your preconceived differences fade away and your commonalities take their place. "Making the first move isn't easy," admitted Michele. "Remember: our default is self-preservation. This is the permanent first hurdle we have to overcome." Commenting on our society and culture more broadly, she went on to add, "There is no doubt that democracy is one of humanity's greatest ideals. It's critical that we don't all think alike. However, we do have to fundamentally think the same about one thing; we have to agree that there is value in every person. The first step to this agreement is noting that there is a stark difference between looking at someone and looking up to someone, and then choosing the latter as our default."[35]

Today we can still choose to react, letting our unconscious be the only governor over our behavior. Or we can choose to move beyond our preconceived notions about one another, however well-fed by our culture, and find reasons to support our deepest understanding that each person has value and deserves our respect.

# I AM YOU ARE WE

## THERE IS NO THEM, THERE IS ONLY US

After my travels across the country, I arrived at Penn's campus in Philadelphia for my freshman year in the fall of 1984. Upon arriving, I discovered I had been placed in a very unusual freshman living arrangement, one that has shaped the rest of my life.

Given an overflow of incoming freshmen, our freshmen group had been placed on the upper floors of the W.E.B. Du Bois College House. The mission of the Du Bois House, named after the remarkable African American social theorist of the early twentieth century, was to support students of the African diaspora by serving as a hub for activities that promote African and African American scholarship and culture.

For reasons I don't completely understand even thirty-five years later, I embraced this environment, which was totally different from the white working-class town of my upbringing. As my wife, Jean, observed in an interview for our campaign launch video, "As is usually the case, everyone would stick to hanging out with their own groups. And because the lobby and the first two floors of the Du Bois House were occupied by African American students, the freshman students would naturally tend to congregate on the upper floors of the building. But not John. He would interact with everybody."

And so that relationship network grew. It seemed entirely natural to me that, at the suggestion of a friend who was the son-in-law of the gospel choir president, I would join the Bible study group for Penn's gospel choir. I also then joined the gospel choir itself, although no white people were among its seventy-five members, and frankly, I couldn't sing all that well. I could obviously tell it was unusual to the rest of the world (I was the only white guy up there!), but it felt right to me.

And so sometime later, when brothers of two historically black fraternities encouraged me to consider pledging, that didn't feel unnatural either.

I plowed ahead and, motivated by the great Alpha Phi Alpha heroes Martin Luther King Jr. and Jesse Owens (among many others), I decided to pledge Alpha. And remarkably, the brothers of the chapter decided to have me.

Many of you probably have never seen a black fraternity pledge class. It is a remarkable sight to behold. The pledge class, called a "line," uniformly has hair stripped nearly to the scalp, dresses in the same paramilitary attire (for us it was boots, black jeans, black hoodies) you wear all

My Alpha Phi Alpha line brothers and me
in 1987—that's me on the far left!

the time, and can't speak to anyone publicly or privately for the seventy-some-odd days you are in the pledging process.

And perhaps most remarkably, you are literally in a "line" for the entire process, shortest to tallest, nose to the back of the shorter person's neck, marching double-time in military fashion and with military-style ninety-degree right turns wherever you might be (in our case, generally Penn's campus, although our travels took us to various black universities up and down the East Coast).

The whole thing may seem awfully strange to outsiders, but I have a lot of respect for the tradition. For this period you pare away expressions of individuality and create a team or squad defined by togetherness. (Recall that the young men in William's wilderness experience also had uniform clothing.) This also applied to how the line functioned together. As in the film *Fight Club*, the first rule of hazing is you don't talk about hazing. But I will temporarily break the rule. In my case, the hazing experience was most terrifying when brothers would come from other schools in the region to haze our line. From their perspective, the obvious question was, Who is this white boy pledging our fraternity, and is he legit? Then they'd test me physically and mentally to find their answer.*

Look, I totally got it; it was a completely reasonable question. I just didn't like having to provide the answer, late night after late night.

A truism of the pledging process is that no one likes the pledging process. But to that I will add that, personally, given these circumstances, I *really* didn't like the pledging process. Some large part of me wanted to curl up in the fetal position and hope the whole thing would just go away.†

---

\* Given I was the tallest, I was last in the line ("number nine") and was therefore more vulnerable in the hazing process. I want to give a special shout-out to the guy in front of me, Rodney Gillespie, one of the most amazing and admirable men I have ever known and someone who worked *very hard* to protect me.

† Against this backdrop, there emerged some unusual villains and saviors. A surprising entry in the "villain" category is my then-girlfriend-now-wife, Jean. Knowing I was always on edge from the hazing, Jean thought it would be hilarious to wake me in the dorm room in the middle of the night with accomplices in bank robber hose-over-face attire and scared the life out of me! That was a good lesson to always watch your "six" (in military terms) because you never know who is after you—even your wife-to-be!

**Our line—together in 2020, at the 100th anniversary
of the chapter. Love these brothers!**

Luckily, it didn't go away, and I didn't quit. I discovered that I can overcome far more fear and pain than I thought possible. Though my line brothers and I came from vastly different worlds, we had more in common than all the things that might separate us. Parts of me were unlocked in that season, parts I never knew but that had always been there. It was truly in this remarkable "we" that I learned more about "me."

Crossing lines of race, culture, and experience brought me into lives, homes, and understandings that have enriched my life tremendously. What I now know is that on the other side of the temporary pain of that pledging season was the promise of more—more discovery, more belonging, more clarity about identity and purpose. And without that experience, I would never be in the place I stand today—seeing those who are often unseen, not taking for granted the authentic diversity of my close friends and family group, and recognizing the value and validity of experiences far removed from my own.

Though I am generally considered a conservative,* when I ran for the Senate in Massachusetts, I decided to announce my campaign at the Edward M. Kennedy Institute for the United States Senate in Boston. The institute honors Ted Kennedy, one of Massachusetts's most famous and revered liberal statesman, and includes a full-scale replica of the United States Senate Chamber. I wanted the voters to know I was willing to take my message of unity to every part of the state, even the place named after "liberal lion" Kennedy himself.

I stood before a chamber full of nearly five hundred friends and supporters, people from all parties and from across the racial and ethnic spectrum. As I shared earlier, one thing about my campaign that I am deeply proud of is that it looked and felt like no political campaign in history. In my campaign management team, we were black and white and Latino and Asian. My management team was comprised of Democrats, Independents, Green Party members, and yes, even Republicans (which I ran as).

I created this campaign team, despite tremendous resistance, because this is America. I wanted the original vision of America to be represented in that remarkable room as I stood under the inscribed Latin phrase *e pluribus unum*, which translates to "Out of the many, we are one." Even the oft-critical *Boston Globe* noted the remarkable diversity and said my campaign announcement made other announcements look "definitely déclassé."[1]

The goal wasn't to outclass my fellow opponents. I wanted my speech and the politically and ethnically diverse crowd to launch my vision for America, one that was decidedly different from the polarizing messages

---

* At least back when that description meant something I could believe in and stand by. My version of conservative counts as its followers figures as disparate as Abraham Lincoln, Frederick Douglass, Ronald Reagan, Jackie Robinson, and Martin Luther King Jr. What customarily passes for "conservative" in national politics and discourse today doesn't look like what I believe in.

of our Republican and Democratic leaders. I wanted nothing more than to be able to talk to my neighbors about the big issues of life, to end up on a debate stage with Senator Elizabeth Warren, and to share the "uniting America" values that I believed critical to our nation's health and survival. As you already know, I wasn't given that opportunity. But in the process of trying, I learned that people of every political, religious, and social context largely have the same desires and share the same objectives.

Whether someone is white and a red "Make America Great Again" hat-wearing individual or black and a card-carrying Black Lives Matter member, I have found that people generally want the same things.

We want a sense of safety and security.

We want opportunity, and even more so, we want opportunity for our children.

We want freedom to express who we are and what we believe in.

Almost everyone I have encountered in my years on this planet—and

My dear friend Reverend Ray Hammond with me
at the 2018 Senate campaign kickoff.

particularly in these last years in public life as I have done hundreds (if not thousands) of meetings with people in my state and around the country—believes deeply in the American ideal of "out of the many, we are one."

What I can tell you now—without an ounce of doubt—is that we are never without hope in this country; there are still far more of us who want to be together than those who want to be apart.

## Maslow and Transcendence

As we discussed earlier, there have been near-constant efforts through the ages to provide comprehensive explanations of who we are, how we are wired, and what it all means for us as people.

Abraham Maslow, one of the most celebrated psychologists in history, offered one such model. He's known as one of the fathers of "humanistic psychology," which differentiated itself from behavioral psychology, practiced by those such as B. F. Skinner. Skinner believed we could be best understood, and in turn altered, through the main stimuli that motivate us to act; "if you change the stimuli, you change behavior" is a key Skinner premise. Maslow believed Skinner's work was too dependent on animal research and didn't account for the distinctiveness of human thought, reason, and language. Most fundamentally, Maslow believed Skinner's approach downplayed the critical role of *choice* for human beings.

Maslow's humanistic psychology also differentiated itself from psychodynamic psychology, practiced by those such as Sigmund Freud, who believed our thoughts and behavior were ultimately determined by the instinctive force of our unconscious—the catalyst for the instantaneous reactions we discussed in the previous chapter. Maslow felt this did not account for the uniqueness of our individual experiences and, most importantly, how each of us translates our experience, which in turn is grounded upon our perceptions and understanding of the world.

How then do we perceive and understand the world we live in? What is the lens we look through to gain understanding about where this journey is headed and what it's all about?

Maslow's most important contribution to humanistic psychology was his 1943 paper titled "A Theory of Human Motivation," which focused on how humans meet their most important needs. At some point you've probably come across some illustrated version of the original "hierarchy of needs" first presented in that paper.[2]

Maslow's hierarchy went viral almost immediately, at least in the mid-twentieth-century meaning of the phrase. Because it was a simple-to-follow pyramid, with the pinnacle being the fulfillment of individual potential, it was gobbled up by corporate America and used liberally as a training tool in human resources. As often happens when we sink our teeth into a handy personal growth tool, Maslow's original hierarchy was never allowed to evolve along with Maslow's own research and thinking. People effectively "locked down" the initial version of Maslow's hierarchy with its pinnacle of "individual fulfillment," even though he would go on to refine and change it over the next three decades.

Maslow's inspiration for the famous hierarchy came when he paid a visit to his anthropologist friends Fritz Lenel, Jane Richardson Hanks, and Lucien Hanks, who were doing research on a Blackfoot Indian reservation in Alberta, Canada.[3] Maslow spent time with the tribal leaders, and through an interpreter he learned about the Blackfoot way of life. According to Cindy Blackstock, an award-winning indigenous scholar and activist, Maslow's notion of ascending needs and the pyramid shape were derived from a combination of the wisdom of the Blackfoot elders and the shape of Blackfoot tepees.[4] As Sarena Johnson of Canada's Student Affairs Exchange has described the tepees, they "depict a similar hierarchy, from the mushrooms struggling in the dirt along the bottom to the celestial beings depicted at the apex."[5]

There is a critical difference, however, between the Blackfoot hierarchy and Maslow's original hierarchy, as both Blackstock and Johnson point out. In the Blackfoot tradition, the idea of self-actualization (a person's pursuit of their full potential) sits at the bottom of the tepee. The second level up is known as community actualization, or a community's pursuit of its full potential. And then at the tip, reaching to the sky, is what Blackstock calls "cultural perpetuity." In other words, the Blackfoot people believed that for a culture to thrive, the individuals within that culture first had to offer their full potential for the sake of the larger community's full potential. When everyone embraces that dynamic, the tribe is able to thrive in perpetuity.

Years after his original pyramid made him famous, Maslow added a new layer to the pinnacle of his pyramid: the concept of "transcendence." He found what the Blackfoot people had known all along, that the highest need we have as humans is for our lives to transcend our individual experience for the sake of a shared one.

**Transcendence is at the top of Maslow's hierarchy of needs.**

**Self-Transcendence**
Seeks to further a cause beyond the self and to experience a communion beyond the boundaries of the self through peak experience
— Self-Transcendent needs

**Self-Actualization**
achieving one's potential as an individual, including creative activities
— Self-fulfillment needs

**Esteem needs**
Seeks esteem through recognition or achievement. Prestige and feeling accomplishment.

**Belongingness and love needs**
Seeks affiliation with a group. Intimate relationships, friends
— Psychological needs

**Safety needs**
Seeks security through order and law
— Basic needs

**Physiological needs**
Seeks to obtain the basic necessities of life: food, water, warmth, rest

Koltko-Rivera, M. (2006) "Rediscovering the Later Version of Maslow's Hierarchy of Needs: Self-Transcendence and Opportunities for Theory, Research, and Unification." *Review of General Psychology* 10, no. 4, 302–17. http://www.koltkorivera.com/psychology.

## The Radical Us!

If you haven't noticed by now, some might find me a bit of an odd duck. I have been wrestling with these matters of who we are and who we should be *together* for nearly my entire life. For example, let me share one story from childhood.

I attended a fundamentalist and legalistic church as a boy. You probably know the type—as in the old movie *Footloose*, you couldn't listen to music, you couldn't dance, and boys and girls were treated very differently. I recall one Sunday when I was nine years old: I found myself in a theological argument of sorts with an elder of our church about "mixed-race marriage" of all things. He shared his theological conviction that it was God's will that people of different races shouldn't marry, which, even as a fourth grader, didn't hold water with me. If memory serves, I was troubled and used my best nine-year-old argument skills, along the lines of, "Wait! What? There's no way the God of the universe that I know would actually think that's a valid principle. That makes no sense to me." And here I am, forty-five years later, still trying to work out the answers to these types of questions.

As I have worked on the principles for this book, I have had the pleasure and privilege of collaborating with some of the smartest and most wonderful people I have ever known. One, a longtime friend and tremendous philosopher-theologian, helped me see something that for me has been hidden in plain sight all along.

As you undoubtedly know, the major monotheistic religious traditions use pretty much the same story of our creation. Something along the lines of: "And God said, 'Let us make human beings in our image, to be like us!'"

The amazing concept that God made humankind in God's own image has informed so much of our religious thought through the ages.

And most of us—whether in faith traditions or not—are familiar with this creation account. But it became more interesting when I realized God refers to "God-self" in this Judeo-Christian version of the creation story (the Muslim version is a little different) using the plural pronouns *us* and *our*. "Let us make human beings in our image, to be like us." The Jewish writer understood that God is all we can possibly imagine and so much more! God is all truth, beauty, knowledge, power, and beyond. Therefore, the singular pronoun can't hold the totality of who God is. So when God talks to God-self, God has to say "us"!

If you are familiar with the Christian concept of the Trinity, you will see where this unusual use of pronouns takes us. In the "three-person" God, there is an affirmation of a God who exists in community. God is a radical "us"!

When God makes humanity in God's image, we reflect God best when we are a radical yet beautiful "us." No one of us captures the image and likeness of God completely. No one individual has "all knowledge" or possesses "all beauty." No one human being contains "all truth" or has "all the answers." While each individual has a fundamental value and dignity that come from God, no one individual reflects the best of God's creation by himself or herself.

Let's put this in real terms for a moment. In his blazing speed, Usain Bolt, the great Jamaican sprinter, captures one facet of who God is. Albert Einstein, with his extraordinary, abstract mind, reflects another facet. Beyoncé, in her singing and dancing and artistic imagination, captures yet another. And so on and so on, through every remarkable character we have discussed in this book and even every person you have ever known!

So no one person is alone the "image of God"—but together, collectively, we are made in the image of God. If you can fully wrap your heart and head around that, it has the power to change everything. I am not fast, but I can glory in Bolt's speed; I am not wired like Einstein, but I can in some way enjoy and participate in his intellectual firepower; and obviously, I don't have Beyoncé's skills, but she too shows me a part of who God is.

You also have your part to contribute to that big reality. The idea of us together reflecting the image of God starts to make greater sense of the words of Jesus, who told us that all the principles of all time are summarized in loving God and loving your neighbor as yourself.[6] Because we are all joint and equal participants in that transcendent and forever storyline. If we don't take being made collectively in the image of God seriously, we lose sight of our need for one another, and our relationships with one another (and with God) are broken and shattered. And consequently, the less we reflect God, the less human we become.

I know this concept may sound hopelessly Pollyannaish in the world we all live in, with fracture lines everywhere, with division and pain and disagreement. Amid our ordinary state of affairs, in the day-to-day, we have sacrificed the radical us for the radical me. But it doesn't change the fact that our collective creation as expressions of God's image—and therefore our need for each other—is wired into our beings. We ultimately survive and thrive when we realize how desperately we need one another, including and especially those we don't like or agree with. Any of the most important battles—against global pandemics, terrorism, cancer, climate change, and mass shootings, or even just paying our bills as a country—aren't battles that can be won by only one party, one group, or one set of ideas. These colossal struggles will require a radical commitment to one another. A radical search for the other's perspective. A radical understanding that no one person or group has all the answers and that honoring the radical us is the first law of our existence.

The Christian tradition reminds us that we are prewired for a radical us. And our crowning achievement is the re-creation and ultimate fulfillment of a radical us. In the last book of the Christian Bible, in a discussion of what heaven will look like, the author wrote,

> I saw a vast crowd, too great to count, from every nation and tribe and people and language, standing in front of the throne and before the Lamb. They were clothed in white robes and held palm branches in their hands. And they were shouting with a great roar,

"Salvation comes from our God who sits on the throne
and from the Lamb!"[7]

The text reminds us that in the end, God never gives up on humanity. God is determined to get us to the point where we reflect him
through a radical fellowship in an incredible loving community that
has God at the center of everything. The ending of our story is in fact a
redeemed new beginning.

## The Road There

When you invoke the life of Jesus of Nazareth as an example of how to
live, you are going big. *Really* big. As big as you can go.

And all the more so when you discuss his crucifixion. After all, none
of us has the distinction of being known as the Son of God, nor have we
experienced something so challenging and outsized as a public crucifixion.

Yet the road map for experiencing that greater and transcendent
community, the one we are wired for and that is in our hearts, is provided
in that crucifixion example. So let's acknowledge these real constraints
(you really can't get all the way around them) and lean in on the part
where Jesus is also understood to be the Son of Man. If we can for a
moment engage the thought experiment of stripping away his Godlike
qualities, we can potentially imagine him to be just like us. Hard, I know,
but bear with me!

In the garden of Gethsemane, Jesus was abandoned in his deep "I
am going to be betrayed and die" sorrow by the best-intentioned of his
friends. They all fell asleep. His worst-intentioned friend (Judas) turned
him over to the authorities and to his eventual death.

After an unbelievable miscarriage in the judicial process, including a sham trial where an unjust and corrupt religious and legal system
completely laid him out, he was sentenced to die. It turns out there
would be a remarkably quick execution of that sentence; indeed, later
that very day.

Jesus's clothes were stripped away, and he was beaten so badly by the Roman soldiers that by some accounts he became unrecognizable. As he made his march of seeming shame through town, he was spit upon, punched, kicked, and insulted.* He was then nailed to a cross alongside two criminals sentenced to the same death penalty and was set upright to die a slow, six-hour death.

Still with me? This is scene-setting for what follows.

In a single phrase that conveys that Jesus really was like us, he expressed the agony of the ages, one humankind experiences often: "My God, why have you forsaken me?"[8]

We all know some version of that feeling. Betrayed, abandoned, unjustly treated by the legal system, the church, a community, or our friends, experiencing directly the loathing of others—or maybe as it seems in our worst times, the loathing of everyone. We feel so alone and hurt and, in a lot of cases, angry.

Against a backdrop of physical and psychological and spiritual anguish, Jesus offered *the* prayer for the ages: *"Father, forgive them, for they do not know what they are doing."*[9]

This is perhaps the most shocking single sentence of all time.

*They don't know what they are doing.*

What? How could that be? Of course they knew!

In this statement, Jesus tells us that those killing him were not people who were unusually *bad* (although to our minds they were certainly that); instead, given they were people made in the image of God—like we all are—they were marked by being *blind*.

For three years leading up to those words, Jesus had been teaching a new lesson about forgiveness and love to all those around him. One of his disciples had asked him, "How many times do I have to forgive someone?" appealing to the old moral law that placed a ceiling on forgiveness. If you are going to follow my way, Jesus responded, you have

---

\* For you *Game of Thrones* fans out there, it probably looked a lot like the "repentance walk" Cersei Lannister had to make through King's Landing.

to forgive "seventy times seven" times.[10] The disciple was amazed—not because Jesus literally blew up the ceiling to 490 specific forgiveness moments but because he understood what Jesus truly meant. We are to be in a continual state of forgiving others.

Broadening the scope of forgiveness even further, Jesus taught a new commandment as well: "Love your enemies, do good to those who hate you."[11] Jesus asks us not only to maintain a consistent posture of forgiveness but also to extend the forever-forgiving attitude to those perhaps deserving of the label "enemies." Dr. Martin Luther King Jr. echoed this commandment in his sermon "Love in Action," preaching forgiveness in the face of humanity's ignorance and citing slavery and segregation as manifestations of a "tragic blindness."[12] "[Jesus] knew that the old eye for an eye philosophy would end up leaving everybody blind. He did not seek to overcome evil with evil. He overcame evil with good. Although crucified by hate, he responded with a radical love."[13]

I think any normal person would believe that these principles of forgiving and loving your enemies have a ceiling. And no matter how high that ceiling is, abandonment, betrayal, public humiliation, and painful public death—all for trumped-up and unjust reasons—would take you beyond that ceiling. But these new teachings are to reorient how we see everything. Instead of viewing others as enemies, we are to forgive and love them. We are not fundamentally disconnected from one another. We are not entirely separated. We all bear pieces of that "image of God" in ourselves and participate to a degree in that image of God in others.

So we aren't made to overcome, overwhelm, or destroy those who aren't with us, even if they are against us or hurt us, but to forgive and liberate them, which in turn liberates us. Forgiveness liberates the heart of one who has been harmed and opens his or her eyes to see a brother or sister made in the image of God.

***

When our country learned that former Dallas police officer Amber Guyger was sentenced to ten years in prison for the murder of Botham "Bo" Jean, it triggered a host of reactions. In the hallway just outside the courtroom, a group protested that the sentence was too lenient. "No justice, no peace," they chanted. Inside the courtroom, the father, mother, sister, and brother of Bo Jean sat silently. Lead prosecutor Jason Hermus walked over and told them he was sorry. "I can't explain that," he admitted, clearly surprised by the jury's sentence, which represented approximately one-third of the twenty-eight-year prison term his legal team had recommended. Judge Tammy Kemp then gave the Jean family members each an opportunity to deliver a victim impact statement in Guyger's presence.

Brandt Jean, Bo's eighteen-year-old younger brother, took the stand in the now–largely empty and quiet courtroom. Rather than reading a written statement, he spoke slowly and carefully, without notes and from his heart:

> I don't want to say twice or for the hundredth time . . . how much you've taken from us. I think you know that. If you truly are sorry . . . I forgive you. . . . I love you just like anyone else. And I'm not going to say I hope you rot and die, just like my brother did. I personally want the best for you. And I wasn't going to ever say this in front of my family or anyone, but I don't even want you to go to jail. I want the best for you.[14]

Brandt Jean referenced his Christian faith, a faith he shared with his late brother, and shared his remarkable conviction that his brother Bo would want the best for his murderer as well and for her to give her life to God.

Brandt then did something no one expected.

"I don't know if this is possible," he said, wiping a tear from his eye and turning to Judge Kemp, "but can I give her a hug, please? Please?"[15]

When Judge Kemp granted Jean's request, he stepped down from the stand and toward the woman who took his brother's life. Guyger stood and rushed to meet Jean in front of the judge's bench. She was sobbing. The two embraced for a full minute as they exchanged a whispered dialogue unheard by the cameras.[16]

The range of reactions to the trial and this moment reflected our divided country. Some commentators were angry, insisting the outcome was yet another injustice against a man of color in this country, not unlike Trayvon Martin, Michael Brown, Eric Garner, Tamir Rice, and Philando Castile. Others were disappointed, believing the sentence was inadequate, yet at the same time were glad Guyger had been found guilty. Still others defended Guyger and her years as a public servant, admitting she'd acted carelessly but not to the level of a murder charge.

I felt the gamut of emotions as I watched it all, from disbelief to compassion to despondence. But putting aside feelings about the unfairness of it all (so systemic and overwhelming), when my wife and I first heard Brandt Jean's statement and watched their hug, we couldn't hold back our tears. There was something so different about Brandt's extraordinary act, which was observed time and again by a range of public figures and pundits, notwithstanding their feelings about Guyger's conviction and prison term.

"Deeply moved" was how Dallas mayor Eric Johnson described his own response to Jean. "I will never, ever forget."[17]

**Brandt Jean's tearful embrace of his brother's killer, Amber Guyger.**

Dallas County district attorney John Creuzot said he'd never seen anything like it over his thirty-seven-year career.[18]

"I couldn't believe what I was hearing," wrote *Cincinnati Enquirer* opinion editor Kevin Aldridge. "Then, I couldn't believe what I was seeing. I sat motionless, mouth agape. . . . I'd like to think my response would be the same as Brandt's . . . but I can't say for sure that it would be."[19]

Many, like Reverend Bernice King, the youngest child of Dr. King, appropriately warned that Brandt Jean's extraordinary gesture should not be mistaken for absolution of Guyger or of those in our country responsible for discrimination and injustice. King is correct that expressing admiration and even hope in the aftermath does not in any way mitigate or excuse our country's history of cruelty, inequality, and injustice. But there was also a common refrain of awe, inspiration, and hope.

As I thought further about it, I came to understand what was so different. Brandt hadn't reacted out of his anger and pain, as completely justified as that would have been. He had seen the image of God in his brother's killer and that in a transcendent way they were more connected than separate. Brandt saw that Guyger needed forgiveness and needed love and that God loved her.

We are, together, made in the image of God. We thrive when we choose to see beyond the many differences and limitations of others. If we are truly honest, the limitations make "them"—whoever they are— exactly like us. We thrive when we are forgiving and accepting and loving.

# CHAPTER 9

# TOGETHER WE WILL AWAKEN AMERICA

## FULFILLING OUR PROMISE

*We hold these truths to be self-evident, that all men are created equal, that they are endowed by their Creator with certain unalienable Rights, that among these are Life, Liberty and the pursuit of Happiness.*

No, it isn't a publishing error that we are repeating this statement from the Declaration, which launched us in chapter 2.

There we discussed the "pursuit" principle, which was part of a truly radical redefinition of the baseline concept of rights. But more revolutionary still was the concept that "all are created equal." Many thousands of books have been written on all the historical roots of this idea and how it came to be embedded in our founding document, but we will only briefly describe what made this such an amazing development.

For tens of thousands of years, the world was principally comprised of tribal cultures, where, more or less, everyone lived nearly all their lives in the same "people category." That certainly didn't ensure legal equality given class, caste, and aristocratic systems, but it did ensure that for the most part, you were all of the same homogeneous group with the same core values. When different "people categories" encountered one another, or when people with conflicting interests in the same category encountered each other, the typical interaction was some imposition of raw power on one another.* At some point along the historical path, governments were organized to apply increasingly rational rules to minimize the extent to which conflicts of interest were addressed only through the use of brute force.

But until the Declaration, all governments had discriminated among people categories. There was no aspiration to do otherwise; it was just the way the systems were constructed.

In the Declaration, for the first time in human history, the governing principle is that we are all equal. Amazing!

But we know that this supposed principle was set against the real lived experience of women, who were largely excluded from these promises of the Declaration. Also, slaves and Native Americans (and no doubt others) were of course entirely excluded, creating a cruel and tragic irony.

On the one hand, in the Declaration we had the greatest governing aspiration ever articulated.

On the other, we had the on-the-ground realities of harsh and barbarous inequality.

Thomas Jefferson, who was the acclaimed author of the Declaration text *and* a notorious slave owner, himself recognized this conflict when he observed the following in 1781: "Indeed, I tremble for my country when I reflect that God is just; that his justice cannot sleep forever."[1]

In his award-winning book *In the Matter of Color*, Judge A. Leon Higginbotham Jr. offered great insight on this terrifically incongruous state of affairs. He asked whether this profound statement in the Declaration is "a self-evident lie, or a self-evident truth."† How could it be so inclusionary in its appeal to the inalienable rights afforded to us by our Creator and so inherently exclusionary at the same time?

---

\* The "state of nature" as discussed at length by the Enlightenment political philosophers. In Thomas Hobbes's *Leviathan*, he writes, "The condition of man . . . is a condition of war of every one against every one, in which case every one is governed by his own reason." And in *Two Treatises of Government*, John Locke states that human nature allows people to be selfish despite being characterized by reason and tolerance.

† He echoes the language of Abraham Lincoln in 1855, who used the same phrases.

I had the tremendous privilege of studying with Judge Higginbotham, and later clerking with him.* He was an enormous African American man (he was listed as six feet six, and I bet he weighed in at nearly three hundred pounds—although I never asked!) with a big booming voice and an infectious laugh (against the backdrop of his huge bass voice, his soprano giggle was surprising and delightful). He had overcome extraordinary hurdles to become a great judge and professor. As Senator Bob Casey recounted in commemorating Higginbotham on the US Senate floor in 2008,

> At age 16 in 1944, Leon enrolled in the engineering program at Purdue University, where the student body had 6000 white students and 12 black students. Leon and his 11 fellow students were required to live in the unheated attic of a campus building. As autumn became winter, snow found its way through the flimsy roof, and the 12 students shivered their nights away, wearing earmuffs, shoes and multiple layers of clothing to bed. As the Midwestern winter grew colder, Leon requested a meeting with the university president to negotiate for a warmer place to sleep, noting that all of the white students slept in heated dormitories. The president responded, "Higginbotham, the law doesn't require us to let colored students in the dorm. We will never do it, and you either accept things as they are or leave the university immediately."[2]

No matter who you are, black, white, Latino, Asian, or what side of this American experience you come from, Higginbotham's experience is kind of a mind-bender. What do you do when the discrepancy between a stated ideal and the degree of commitment to an ideal is so great? Do you just scrap the ideal entirely because the people who wrote it obviously

---

* I have frequently been the so-called "conservative" thinker in these so-called "liberal" rooms. I taught Harvard undergraduates with another legendary professor, Robert Coles, and there was a similar dynamic there. Nevertheless, I have always found the areas of agreement in the more liberal clerking and teaching fellow rooms (under the watch of these great men) to be much greater than the areas of disagreement. We would hold the same anchoring principles in common, while at times disagreeing about how to best achieve our shared objectives in practice.

didn't mean it (since they were living lives entirely opposite of the aspiration)? And given that Higginbotham had experienced the consequences of that personally, wasn't he deeply dispirited?

As he worked to resolve that question, Judge Higginbotham would quote the words of one of the most famous US Supreme Court justices, Benjamin Cardozo. Justice Cardozo described "the tendency of a principle to expand itself to the limit of its logic."[3]

In the view of Higginbotham and others, the words "all men are created equal" in the Declaration created the largest possible promise in our first statement as a nation, a promise that demanded, ultimately, that it be fulfilled. This became the standard to be appealed to, and ultimately fulfilled in, the Emancipation Proclamation freeing the slaves, the Fourteenth Amendment's guarantee of the equal protection of the laws (for the newly freed slaves and otherwise), the Twentieth Amendment's guarantee of the right of women to vote, the Civil Rights Act of 1964, and beyond. Lincoln described the work of Jefferson and the framers of the Declaration as "meant to set up a standard maxim for free society, which should be . . . constantly looked to, constantly labored for, and even though never perfectly attained, constantly approximated, and thereby constantly spreading and deepening its influence, and augmenting the happiness and value of life to all people of all colors everywhere."[4]

Notwithstanding all the barbarity and cruelty and loss of life in America before these promises came to be fulfilled, and having experienced a fair bit of injustice himself, Judge Higginbotham believed that the original statement of the as-yet-unfulfilled ideal was a very good thing. While cynicism or bitterness might be a normal response, Judge Higginbotham remained ever hopeful.

## Fulfilling Our Promise

Among Judge Higginbotham's many remarkable achievements, he worked to transition South Africa to free democratic elections and helped the newly elected government draft a new constitution. Let's step back to make sure we are keeping track of the historical thread here—because it gets a little complicated, but it is worth following.

1. Our founders created a principle for a free society.
2. That promise remained unfulfilled for a very long time.
3. In his lifetime, Judge Higginbotham himself experienced that unfulfilled promise.
4. Notwithstanding these challenges, Judge Higginbotham went on to assume the mantle of advancing that promise and principle for all Americans.
5. Even further, Judge Higginbotham carried forward the best of that American promise to assist in the freedom of South Africa.

Along the way, he worked closely with one of the most remarkable of all leaders, Nelson Mandela.

The life and experiences of Mandela are legendary. As a boy, Mandela listened to the elders' stories of his ancestors' valor during the wars of resistance, dreaming of making his own contribution to the freedom struggle of his people. Mandela became arguably the central figure in the struggle against South Africa's brutal apartheid regime. Demonstrating almost unimaginable patience and perseverance, he spent twenty-seven years in the darkness of a prison cell. He was then elected president of South Africa in the democratic election that Higginbotham assisted with, making Mandela the country's first black president. Mandela then presided over the extraordinarily challenging transition from apartheid to multiracial democracy through his plan of national reconciliation.

While facing the death penalty in the Rivonia Trial in 1964, Mandela famously decided not to testify on his own behalf. He instead shared a statement "from the dock" (the enclosed area the accused sits in during a trial) lasting over three hours, closing with the now-storied words reflecting his anchoring commitments: "I have fought against white domination, and I have fought against black domination. I have cherished the ideal of a democratic and free society in which all persons live together in harmony and with equal opportunities. It is an ideal which I hope to live for and to achieve. But if needs be, it is an ideal for which I am prepared to die."[5]

His story is among the most epic of the modern era. His opponents imprisoned him *for decades*, and then he came out to lead not only his "people category" but also those who imprisoned him to a more perfect union.

Judge Higginbotham can't quite touch those extraordinary heights (who can?), but in his life there were meaningful echoes of Mandela.

**Nelson Mandela leaving the courtroom in Pretoria during the Treason Trial in 1958.**

Despite the tremendous adversity Higginbotham had experienced, he was kind and wise. To me personally, and in all the interactions I ever witnessed—in the classroom, in the courtroom, in the chambers, and otherwise—he was strong yet gentle.* Judge Higginbotham helped craft sensible constitutions for nations around the world, most notably across Africa. In my relatively short clerkship period in 1992, delegations of legal scholars from two African nations came to meet with the judge and his clerks to receive the benefit of his guidance in forming their constitutions.

To put this into perspective, 1992 was:

- 216 years after the declaration of that imperfect yet wonderful aspiration—"All are created equal."
- 127 years after the end of Civil War hostilities, with the loss of nearly seven hundred thousand American lives fighting over the "all created equal" principle.
- 48 years after young Higginbotham was freezing in the Indiana winter at Purdue, denied warm quarters to sleep in given the color of his skin.
- 28 years after the Civil Rights Act.

---

*      One funny story about the "strong" part of Judge Higginbotham. When I was a young student in his class, we did a mock trial rearguing the 1954 *Brown v. Board of Education* case (often described as a "moot court" in the legal education world, but this was in my undergraduate years). It was daunting enough to imagine doing this in front of Judge Higginbotham in any setting, but he took us off campus to do this in his courthouse at the Third Circuit Court of Appeals—a really important court! I had dressed myself as "fancy" and formal as a college-age student with my modest upbringing could manage, and I stepped into the courtroom for my presentation. I started with, "May it please the court," the standard courtroom protocol that we had been instructed to lead with, and launched in. Judge Higginbotham almost immediately interrupted me with his near "voice of God" filling the courtroom, calling me to an apparent error at the outset. "Counsel, I see that you haven't . . ." he began, calling me out on what he believed to be an error in my protocol and approach. Unbeknownst to the Judge, I had carefully followed the written instructions of his teaching fellows, and he was now conveying the exact opposite instruction in correcting me. I was trapped! Do I correct the Judge in correcting me, or do I proceed? I don't think I ever fully recovered in my oral presentation as I shakily proceeded to its completion.

As a nation, we were slowly working out the fulfillment of our founding principle. And Judge Higginbotham was doing his part, working faithfully and fully to advance it, and doing so in the very best American tradition, for various people categories in our nation (including lowly students like me) and for people categories around the world. I believe we are at our best in our country when we wrestle together to sort these aspirations and principles and advance them in our own land—and then, as with Judge Higginbotham, work to share that with others around the world.

As Mandela himself observed while commenting on Higginbotham's remarkable contributions to a democratic and constitutional South Africa, "Judge Higginbotham's work and the example he set made a critical contribution to the rule of law in the United States and a difference in the lives of African-Americans, and indeed the lives of all Americans."[6] Rosa Parks observed after Higginbotham's funeral, "I think he really had a great idea that we are all equal people."[7]

In short, as Mandela led all South Africans as justly and wisely as could be done, Higginbotham led all Americans, and many Africans, justly and wisely.

Their lives of public service embody nearly all the principles we have discussed.

Knowing their purpose notwithstanding their circumstances? Check.

Doing more with less? Check again.

Redeeming adversity? And how!

Understanding that we are generally alike, and responding accordingly? The cornerstone of their lives and work.

But perhaps their most profound commitment was to a transcendent community, to the truth that we were made for one another and that we complement one another.

On that basis, they forgave their transgressors fully, helping them overcome their blindness and liberating them, which in turn was liberating for Mandela and Higginbotham.

After the end of my campaign, the backbone of our black/white/Latino/ Asian team stayed together to figure out how to keep working to advance our mission beyond the political arena. We are committed to awakening America to the forgotten foundations of who we are and who we are meant to be. Recall from the opening chapters that even holding aside the effects of the coronavirus, nearly 150,000 suicides and overdoses occur per year—an unprecedented and staggering number—and measures of anxiety, depression, loneliness, and isolation are spiking in every demographic.

Drawing from the same principles that informed the Better for America campaign in 2016 and the Uniting America and the Senate campaigns in 2017–2018, we are now committed to a new campaign. We are calling this movement American Awakening—for reasons that after 171 pages I hope are obvious to you! We are using any means available to us—leading first with books, daily livestreams and podcasts, film, concerts, and immersive entertainment experiences—to slay the giant of death and despair in this American moment.

One of my favorite quotations is from the great African American nineteenth-century statesman Frederick Douglass. He said, "I would unite with anyone to do right and with nobody to do wrong."[8] Our team's efforts are anchored in that principle, and so one initiative is dedicated to bringing together individuals and organizations who are standing against this present darkness.

Last November our team hosted our first two "unite with anyone to do what is right" gatherings of national thought and spiritual leaders at the Vermont farm. Our commitment was that these rooms would be filled with black, white, Latino, and Asian Americans across generations, ranging across all theological, political, and governing philosophies (Republican, Independent, Libertarian, Democrat, Green) and including artists, entertainers, entrepreneurs, academics, writers, clergy, and activists. Beyond their being leaders in their spheres, the only criteria was that their life stories had demonstrated that they were also committed to standing against the death and despair of the day.

One of our family dogs, Ranger, was with us. He had an unusual accident just before the second weekend that I didn't think much of at the time. He was running and jumping like dogs always do, merely doing "dog stuff," and dislocated his back right hip. While we normally leave our dogs in the care of others and don't impose them on our company, in this case, we felt like we needed to keep him close and in our care after his surgery. My wife, Jean, sensed that he was being a constant distraction to the group, which as a host made her very uncomfortable.

In spite of Ranger's injuries, we pressed on. For two consecutive weekends, this remarkable array of individuals flew into Boston from across the country and then shuttled three hours to this quintessential small New England town. Our opening-night welcome receptions were filled with intrigued adventurers wondering who we were, how we had found them, and what exactly we had in store.

We introduced our American Awakening work and highlighted the work our guests are doing to shift darkness into light. Both weekends were memorable—the wonderful professional musicians, colorful personalities, stirring worship, midnight group singalongs, and powerful nontraditional closing Eucharist ceremonies will long remain etched in our collective memories. But the second weekend was especially powerful.

I joked at our opening session that Vermont had never before seen a room of such strong African American women. The statement was probably accurate—from prominent national voices to next-gen social entrepreneurs and activist clergy, the room was filled with a cultural clarity, grace, and strength notably influenced by these women and their experiences and perspectives. The conversations on experiences of race and gender in the Christian world were intense from the beginning. The atmosphere in the room felt heavy as various guests of color described their feelings of deep alienation and tremendous pain resulting from experiences in oft-exclusionary, white, male-dominated circles of faith. And the feelings were hard earned and understandable, given their circumstances and experiences. Several guests were unsure whether they had any place within the church, a sentiment they expressed with great sadness.

I will be honest; as the host, I wasn't entirely sure how to handle this. I have experienced many strong expressions of the pain resulting from hundreds of years of tortured racial history, but in this room there seemed to be an unusual degree of freedom, and our guests spoke more directly on these topics than I had ever heard.

When we were together in the meeting room on the final day, the potential fracture lines seemed obvious. The wary suspicion and deep frustration challenged our commitment to radical togetherness.

When we reached the heaviest point in the conversation, one of our teammates, Marisa, leaned forward and spoke for the first time that day. Marisa is an accomplished black woman, a film *and* law school graduate, the producer of all our American Awakening projects, and the leader of our team. In the stillness of the moment, she spoke from her own experience of injustice and wounding, which can't be minimized or wished away. But she had come to recognize there is something larger at work than the pain she has experienced and the obvious limitations of some of our social structures—and that as children of God, we have a choice.

Do we remain mired in despair, or do we believe that we were made by God for a purpose that is unique to each of us and our lives, and can therefore experience peace and power and rest?

Do we remain anxious that there isn't enough for us, or do we believe that the God of the universe has provided for us and the purpose we were made for?

Do we remain captive to adversity we have faced, or do we use and triumph over it and believe that it has forged us into the people we were meant to be?

Because we know who we are as children of God and who we were made to be, we have the freedom to choose.

I was personally stunned by the clarity and insight of her words, but the room fell quiet for what seemed an eternity. I frankly wasn't sure whether this moment marked the end of this "radical togetherness" experiment!

In the near-deafening silence that followed, one of the most respected activist voices in the room (we will call her Melody) offered what seemed to be a breakthrough reflection. Interestingly, and unbeknownst to Jean and me, Melody had been closely observing Ranger all weekend. Given the injury, one leg had been put in a sling of sorts, and therefore Ranger had been walking around on three legs. She'd assumed that he'd been injured for some time and had learned to cope and adapt over weeks or months. When Melody realized it was a fresh injury that occurred merely hours before the start of the weekend, but he was still sprinting around in full-on dog fashion—like the injury hadn't slowed him down at all—she was struck. "I know a lot of us in this work, we're deeply connected to the problems. We feel the pain, and we definitely know the hurt. But I'm

Ranger, just after surgery and on his way to
our American Awakening gathering.

here watching Ranger. He knows he's injured, but he's not letting that stop him. He's not even limping. It's really kind of beautiful. I can't help but think there might be something in that for us."

The mood in the room immediately shifted. Given Melody's keen observation and Ranger's resilience, we had a model for who we were supposed to be together. We may be injured, often by others or by circumstances with parts of us bandaged up or even in slings, but we are to engage with one another fully, ultimately not letting our injuries slow us at all.

In a newsletter and online posting last year, hedge fund manager Drew Dickson uncharacteristically departed from his customary musings about business and finance. Dickson shared a story about his son, Max, an amazing young man whose demons arrived with a vengeance around the time he was sixteen. "For three years," wrote Dickson, "my wife and I would wait on our front stoop until 5:00 am hoping that he would come home. On those nights that he didn't, we would call the hospitals, and call the police. And sometimes the police would call us."

As any parent would, the Dicksons tried everything they could think of. Over the course of three years, they changed schools, they visited psychologists, and they even tried the wilderness therapy that had been so transformative for my son William.

Nothing helped. Max was drowning in anxiety and depression, and the Dicksons eventually had to face the helpless reality that they couldn't save their son. Only he could choose to live.

Eventually, Max asked his parents if he could leave London, where they were living at the time. He'd taken trips to far-flung destinations before, with little resulting benefit, but he asked again anyway. "He chose a destination a lot of rudderless kids like to visit," Dickson wrote. "It might as well have been Goa, Tulum, Koh Tao or Maui, but he chose Costa Rica. A friend of his, a good guy, was backpacking there, and invited him to come. I told Max we'd cover the first week, but if he wanted to stay longer, he had to get a job and support himself. We honestly didn't know what to expect, but it felt like a last shot for him."

Max found a job working at a hostel, and it seemed, for a brief time, that the move was the best thing for him. But reality eventually set in, and his anxiety and depression returned. The Dicksons feared they wouldn't hear their son's voice again. Then something happened. Max found an eight-week-old puppy wandering the streets of Santa Teresa. The dog ate trash and had obviously been abused. It was frightened of people, but for some reason he wasn't afraid of Max. The two formed an instant bond. Together, Max and "Chica" became inseparable.

Through Chica, Max came to see he had something to offer the world, even if his offering only involved caring for a small puppy. He began saving money, making personal sacrifices so he could take Chica to the vet. As Chica became healthier, Max did too. Dickson began to see the signs that his son who'd struggled for years was starting to come back to life. He could hear it in his voice.

In a phone call when Max was nineteen, he told his dad he was ready to leave Costa Rica. But he didn't want to return to London, where he feared he'd lapse back into old habits. Instead, he wanted to move to Indianapolis. The Dicksons had family there, and they felt relieved knowing that Max would have people who loved him nearby if things turned south again.

But they didn't.

The Dicksons flew to Indianapolis to help Max get settled in his new apartment. Before long, he had a new full-time job and was doing well. As Dickson wrote, "Max had saved Chica. And Chica had saved Max."

Then three months into his newfound life, Max was walking Chica near his downtown apartment when Chica spotted a squirrel. She darted from Max's grip straight onto Indiana Avenue and right in front of a speeding car. The car hit Chica, and Max yelled out and fell to his knees. In a moment, everything he had worked for seemed to be gone.

The driver that hit Chica sped off, but the next car stopped. It was a young African American man not much older than Max. He hopped from the car. "I got you," he said to Max and introduced himself as Kenny.

He held up traffic and walked Max to the middle of the road to retrieve Chica's bloodied body. She was somehow still breathing but badly hurt. Kenny helped Max and Chica into his car and hurried them to a vet clinic. What Max didn't know then was that Kenny himself had just moved to Indianapolis where he'd been hired temporarily but hoped to make the job a permanent gig.

The first vet told Max that Chica needed surgery for a broken pelvis or she would die. But he wasn't a surgeon. Kenny stayed with Max and looked up another vet on his phone and took Max and Chica there. The second vet was able to perform the surgery and save Chica's life. Max then nursed her back to health over the next several months. And once again, as Chica's health improved, Max's did too. Today he's in the best health, physically and emotionally, of his life.

Kenny stayed in touch with Max after that day, checking in to see how Chica was doing and encouraging Max, even taking him to an Indianapolis Colts game and dinner afterward. As a dad of four children myself, I understand Dickson's sentiment when he wrote, "This guy Kenny, I want to reach out and give him the biggest hug he ever got. I want to tell him that he is special. I want to thank him for saving Chica's life. I want to thank him for saving my son's."

As for Kenny, he eventually got that full-time job he'd been hoping for. His full name is Kenny Moore, from Valdosta, Georgia. He signed a contract with the Indianapolis Colts to be the highest-paid slot corner-back in the NFL—a deal that would pay him at least $30 million over the next four years.[9]

When I was on the campaign trail, I often reflected on the spiritual journeys and public lives of Abraham Lincoln, Winston Churchill, and Martin Luther King Jr. Each shared a vision that was unpopular and positioned them well outside the mainstream for a very long time: Lincoln and his vision for America in the 1850s, Churchill and his warnings about Adolf Hitler and the rise of Nazi Germany in the 1930s, and King and his vision of unity in the 1960s. Each anchored their vision in recalling people to the DNA of their countries and cultures, which if followed would create a "radical us" rallying against the profound challenge of their day.

For Lincoln, that was ending slavery and restoring the Union. For Churchill, saving Great Britain from Hitler and the Third Reich. For King, overcoming our systemic injustice and achieving his dream of a land of truly free and equal people. The vision of each was eventually validated, although tragically through tremendous cost to their countries and families and selves. In the case of Lincoln and King, it required the sacrifice of their own lives.

Interestingly, each also had a strong view of the significance of America to the world for both the day they lived in and for the future. In his 1862 State of the Union address, during the darkest days of the Civil War, Lincoln revisited a theme he had explored before—America as the "last best hope" for the world.* Churchill observed that the United States is like a "gigantic boiler. Once the fire is lighted under it there is no limit to the power it can generate."[10]

I could end this book with a range of insights from any of them to speak into the challenges and possible solutions in this American moment, and it would almost invariably be fitting. (You just can't go wrong with these guys!) But I will go with Lincoln, who bookended the Civil War with two remarkable Inaugural addresses. Each reflected his effort to awaken Americans to their truest selves and the profound idea that we are to live fully together.

In his first Inaugural address on the eve of the Civil War, Lincoln

---

* From the concluding remarks of Lincoln's State of the Union Address (December 1, 1862): "Fellow-citizens, *we* cannot escape history. We of this Congress and this administration, will be remembered in spite of ourselves. No personal significance, or insignificance, can spare one or another of us. The fiery trial through which we pass, will light us down, in honor or dishonor, to the latest generation. We *say* we are for the Union. The world will not forget that we say this. We know how to save the Union. The world knows we do know how to save it. We—even *we here*—hold the power, and bear the responsibility. In *giving* freedom to the *slave*, we *assure* freedom to the *free*—honorable alike in what we give, and what we preserve. We shall nobly save, or meanly lose, the last best hope of earth."

offered this encouragement to the nation: "We are not enemies, but friends. We must not be enemies. Though passion may have strained it must not break our bonds of affection. The mystic chords of memory, stretching from every battlefield and patriot grave to every living heart and hearthstone all over this broad land, will yet swell the chorus of the Union, when again touched, as surely they will be, by the better angels of our nature."[11]

For four long years the country was torn apart by the war, which resulted in over one million casualties and nearly seven hudred thousand deaths. To put that loss of life into perspective, a proportionate loss in today's US population of approximately 330 million people would require seven million deaths and ten million total casualties. Against that backdrop, Lincoln's exhortation to find our "better angels" and his assertion that "we are not enemies, but friends" must have been unbelievably bitter and painful. And yet as the war wound to its close—just weeks before its end and his own assassination—Lincoln pressed on with a similar vision for the broken nation: "With malice toward none, with charity for all, with firmness in the right as God gives us to see the right, let us strive on to finish the work we are in, to bind up the nation's wounds, to care for him who shall have borne the battle and for his widow and his orphan, to do all which may achieve and cherish a just and lasting peace among ourselves and with all nations."[12]

Malice toward none! Charity to all! Bind up the nation's wounds! These are encouragements to a nation that are fitting in any season, not just during a civil war.

In this American moment of despair, division, and death (now including effects of the coronavirus), we as a nation and people are in peril. And if you look around carefully, you will find people in your state in peril, people in your city or town in peril, and in all likelihood people in your closest community of friends and loved ones in peril. You may find yourself (or your family) in peril already or, because we are all linked together, likely to be in some peril soon.

As we face these times, we are not enemies; we are friends. We are not just black or white or Latino or Asian—we are Americans. We are not just Right or Left—we are Americans. We are not just straight or gay—we are Americans. We are not just male or female; academically smart, mechanically brilliant, or developmentally challenged; rich or poor—we are Americans. We are not just Republican, Democrat, Green, Libertarian, or Independent; Red state, Blue state, or Purple state; Christian, Muslim, Jew—we are all Americans!

Like Mandela, Judge Higginbotham, Marisa, Melody, Kenny, and Max, we all share relationships with one another that transcend the people categories we are placed in. We are together made in the image of God and are brothers and sisters who need one another.

Your contribution to this story doesn't have to be as epic as Mandela's, as remarkable as Higginbotham's (he was awarded honorary degrees from sixty-two universities and colleges—sixty-two!), or as insightful as Marisa's and Melody's.

But I believe nearly any of us can—like Kenny—see a dog and a young man in pain and stop to help. And perhaps, although we may never fully know, our contribution might change a story, affect a community, influence a town or city, and ultimately maybe even save a state or nation in peril.

It will take courage, as it always does. All the greatest stories require courage from us, and the greater the story, the more courage required.

Yet if we can press on with a dose of courage and play our parts, recollecting our forgotten foundations, I know we can awaken America, fulfill our promise, and together restore the soul of America. And perhaps we can go even further, as Judge Higginbotham did when helping spread what he had learned in this American project to Mandela and South Africa and other nations around the world.

Together we will not only defeat the giant of despair, division, and death in this country but also light a fire under this gigantic American boiler; and perhaps that boiler will generate enough power to provide a beacon of freedom and liberty and opportunity for the rest of the world.

# OUR JOURNEY CONTINUES

A recurring dream nags a young Andalusian shepherd named Santiago in Paulo Coelho's breakout novel *The Alchemist*. Santiago lives the simple life of an ancient outdoorsman; every time he sleeps under a sycamore tree that grows among the ruins of a church, he dreams of a child who tells him to venture to the Egyptian pyramids where a treasure awaits him. Eventually, Santiago sells his flock and sets out for Tangier. The adventure is, like life itself, equal parts mystery, adversity, and discovery.

After Santiago has a premonition that saves a mysterious two-hundred-year-old alchemist from a tribal attack, the old alchemist joins his journey. Arab soldiers attack the two and force Santiago to give up his money; the old alchemist turns lead into gold and leaves it with Santiago before bidding him farewell.

When arriving at the pyramids and digging for his treasure, Santiago is once more accosted and beaten. (Poor Santiago is really having a tough go of it on this journey!) As the attackers leave Santiago, one of them mocks his dream by sharing one of his own; he says it involves a treasure buried beneath a sycamore tree that grows from the ruins of an old church. Santiago stops digging and begins his journey home where he finds that all along a treasure of gold and jewels has been buried beneath the sycamore tree where he slept.

Homecoming is one of the most poignant themes in film, literature, and the grand narratives of history's primary religions. Homecoming accounts in the great stories generally feature a central character who believes that a treasure exists "out there" to be hunted down. Like Santiago, the heroes of these stories discover that the treasure is ultimately to be found at home; but to make that discovery, it seems they have to leave and take a journey in order to find it back where they started.

The great American poet T. S. Eliot described this phenomenon in what is perhaps his most famous poem.

> We shall not cease from exploration
> And the end of all our exploring
> Will be to arrive where we started
> And know the place for the first time.[1]

Jerusalem is the spiritual home for the three great monotheistic religions and over half the people on the planet. Over the last three millennia, the city has been taken or destroyed forty times and rebuilt twenty-five times, which forms a remarkable story of the resilience of a place and peoples over many generations.[2]

On a recent visit (my first!), I sat overlooking the walls of the Old City and was struck by the fact that in many of these great religious traditions, it is believed to be the starting place for all of us—the story of Adam, the beginning of all our stories. And then the greats of each religious tradition appear here. It is where Abraham surrendered Isaac as an offering to God, which provided the baseline for the covenant between God and the Hebrew people; where Jesus appeared before Pontius Pilate and was then crucified and resurrected; and where Muhammad ascended to heaven from the Temple Mount.

Most amazingly of all, there is the belief—most expressly for Jews and Christians but implied for Muslims—that in this place a perfect "home" will be created for us. The Messiah will come and will make a New Jerusalem where all will be right. There will be perfect harmony and concord among all the troubled and warring peoples, and the "wolf will live with the lamb, the leopard will lie down with the goat, the calf and the lion and the yearling together," as the prophet Isaiah told us. And there will be no death or pain or tears.[3]

As these religious traditions teach us, we are wired for that home-coming, and we look forward to that home; until then we are left to do our best to bring that version of our ultimate home into our lives here and now.

———

When I was in high school, a friend casually said to me, "Hey, John, I saw your dad leaving the Purple Cow tavern last week." Seeing my dad leave the Purple Cow was just a cool coincidence to him. It was mind-bending to me. I remember thinking, "Why would my dad be at a tavern if he doesn't drink? He can't drink, according to our faith."

As I shared in the opening of the book, I soon learned he'd been drinking pretty much every day of my life. In his great classic *1984*, George Orwell talked about the terrific and terrible force of taking the simple and plain meaning of things and turning it completely upside down—so in his quintessential example, "black" becomes "white," and "white" becomes "black." When I learned of my dad's alcoholism, my life felt like an Orwellian black-is-white and white-is-black experience—what the thing is called or what you are told is not the thing that is actually happening.

I attribute those circumstances—having the rug of my early reality yanked out from under me—to my lifelong uncertainty about a lot of things. I sometimes call myself "agnostic," but not in the way people normally use it to describe their "not knowing" whether God exists. For me, when I say I'm agnostic, I mean a more general "without knowledge"—the root meaning of the word—which has always forced me to find out the real answers to life's most pressing questions.

All these years on, I feel certain about the most fundamental things in life—God's grace and love, my family's love, my gratitude for this country, the value of the principles in this book—but if I'm being honest, I'm just not sure about a lot of other stuff we often pretend to be sure about.

When I learned that the reality of my childhood wasn't the reality I'd seen and been told, I went through what many of us go through at some point or another; I questioned everything because I wanted to know what was really true, even about myself. All I'd been told in my preadult life was suspended, and I wasn't sure about much of anything. So I set out on that journey to figure out what I could be certain of, if anything. That trip I described in chapter 1 formed a new imprint on my heart and mind, with chapters to continue over the following thirty-six years.

I didn't return home as an eighteen-year-old, newly minted adult with wisdom beyond his years.

I didn't return home to find that my dad was clean and my mom was emotionally well again. I returned home with an understanding that life was complicated but better and bigger and more interesting than I'd ever been told or known.

When I think about my relationships with people, I find I am most drawn to those who have gone through difficulties and emerged on the other side to keep journeying, people who have some scars or pain, as Melody observed about Ranger. Comparatively, my scars are smaller than those of many people. Nevertheless, the truth is that we all have them. And the scars make us more complex and compelling people, more capable of empathy and compassion for one another and more necessary to one another. Our scars and our pain unite us—if we allow that to be the case.

It reminds me of the ancient Japanese art form called Kintsugi, where an artist uses gold lacquer to repair broken ceramics and pottery, making the repaired vessels unique and more beautiful than when they were whole. Legend has it that its beginnings can be traced back to a story about scars.

A Japanese artist spent years painstakingly handcrafting a beautiful ceramic teapot in hopes that good fortune would one day allow him to serve tea to the country's most famous tea man, who lived in a remote village not far from his own. Eventually, that fortune came, and the artist received notice that the famous tea man would come join him for tea in one week's time. When the day arrived, the artist woke early and carefully shined the teapot to perfection as he awaited the tea man's arrival. This famous man arrived and sat on a pillow in the artist's small home awaiting his tea. It was the moment the artist had been waiting for. He handed the tea man a saucer and cup. He then presented the teapot with which he filled the tea man's cup, fully expecting that the man would be overwhelmed by its intricate beauty.

To his surprise and disappointment, the tea man took no notice of the teapot. The artist was so devastated that as soon as the tea man left, he walked deep into the woods behind his home and threw the teapot against a large stone, breaking it into pieces.

Years later an aspiring artist was walking through those same woods when he came across the remnants of the shattered teapot. He saw something in the pieces and gathered them all up and returned to his humble home. There he repaired the teapot using a special golden lacquer that had been passed down from his great-grandfather. When he was finished, the teapot had retaken its original shape but looked quite different, as the cracks between the broken pieces reached like shining golden scars up, down, and around the vessel.

As luck would have it, a few days later, the second artist received a notice that the tea man would come to his home in two days' time. When the day came, like the first artist, the second artist handed the tea man a saucer and cup and began to pour tea into it from the newly repaired teapot. Immediately, the tea man stopped the second artist. He set down his cup and saucer and took the repaired teapot into his hands. "I have never seen something so exquisite in all my years!" he exclaimed. And in that very moment, he entrusted his entire tea fortune to the second artist, as he had only months to live and he'd lost his only child years before.

Shocked, the second artist asked him why he would do such a thing.

The tea man replied, "I've beheld a thousand unbroken teapots and was moved by none. Today you have shown me that the greatest strength and truest beauty lies in our brokenness."[4]

I've thought a lot about the complicated and difficult parts of my life over the last thirty-six years. I used to hope I would someday grow up

185

and leave all that behind. But then I realized I can't and shouldn't. And neither should you. We can't merely forget our past, trying to bury the broken pieces in the dirt of some remote forest. Things have happened to each one of us, and the pieces were strewn on the earth. And yet the broken parts of our lives can become the most beautiful aspects of who we are if we are willing to pick up the pieces and bond them back together with strength, compassion, and ingenuity.

This is as true for you and me as individuals as it is for our communities and our country. We are broken. But we can be stronger and more beautiful than we've ever been.

This is what radical togetherness means. There will be no such thing as "perfect unity" in our lifetime. Although we are wired for that truest homecoming, we won't fully experience it today.

But knowing we are ultimately meant to be together—*together*, when we arrive at that home—we can for now chose unity as broken pieces artfully, willingly bonded back together.

But we can get there only if, together, we never give in. Never, ever, ever.

A Kintsugi teacup. The greatest strength and truest beauty lies in the renewal of our brokenness.

© Lia_t/Shutterstock

# ACKNOWLEDGMENTS

As the great Fannie Lou Hamer (a civil rights leader who doesn't always get her due) observed, never "forget where we came from and always praise the bridges that carried us over."

In that spirit, I want to express my great gratitude to the following (in rough chronological order).

To my mother Jayne Kingston, late father Jack Kingston, and parents-in-law Roy and Madeline Yih: Jean and I so appreciate the tremendous adversity (we know your lives have been very difficult) that you have redeemed. Thank you for doing your very best to instill these values in us.

To my line brothers (chapter 8), fantasy baseball league (chapter 7), guys' group (chapter 6), and the Colorado group (you know who you are!): thank you for living your lives and sharing your highs and lows with me over the better part of these last thirty-five years.

To our children (and their fiancés/spouses), Caitlin (and Andrew), Annalise (and Troy), Christopher, and William: thank you for helping your imperfect dad as he tried (and tries) to figure this out with you in the laboratory of family life! May these principles anchor you as you continue to grow into the compassionate and courageous men and women you are meant to be.

To Reverend Hurmon Hamilton, Reverend Ray Hammond, and Reverend Steve Macchia, as dear of friends, advisors, and partners as anyone could have: thank you for your faith, wisdom, and unwavering commitment to love me so radically and to develop in me the vision shared in this book.

ACKNOWLEDGMENTS

To my Sword & Spoon/Better for America/Kingston for Senate teammates Cathy Fair, Lindsay Flood, and Bill Wall: I cannot do justice to the challenges and burdens you took on and shouldered these last handful of years as we worked together to help this country fulfill its promise. For worse or for better (I hope for the better!), it is because you helped carry me on this journey that I have remained in this great battle to restore the soul of America.

To Marisa Prince and Calvin Lee: every day over the last years, you have contributed your courage and conviction to this vision. Marisa, thank you for being the leader and inspiration of our efforts and true to the remarkable purpose God created you for. Calvin, who knew the "body man" I hired for the Senate campaign three years ago would be such a great visionary and writer (this book wouldn't have gotten done without you!)?

To my American Awakening teammates Joel Searby, Andy Peterson, Jeff Bethke, Cristian Palacios, and Marina Pappas: thank you for your passion and commitment and tireless efforts to make AA's vision a reality.

To Brent Cole and Nancy French: your vision and imagination (and in the case of Nancy, your many decades of friendship) helped make this book a reality, and I thank you for it! And to Dr. Baldwin Way of Ohio State University and Dr. Matthew Lee and Dr. Tyler VanderWeele of Harvard University: thank you for your invaluable guidance in providing us the most up-to-date scientific insights and helping us synthesize them with the "forever" principles we all care so deeply about.

To my wonderful agents, Mike Snider and Margaret Riley King, and the entire WME team: thank you for your partnership in this initiative to stand against death, despair, and division in this American moment.

To my publisher, David Morris, and the rest of the HarperCollins team, Alicia Kasen, Andy Rogers, Kim Tanner, Robin Barnett, Andrea Kelly, and Dale Williams: thank you for believing in the renewal and restoration of our great land and your patience and professionalism at every turn.

To David Brooks and Anne Snyder and Arthur Brooks (all the

important Brooks I know!): thank you for your friendship and your visionary leadership. And to David and Anne: the version of "John Kingston" you kindly described in the foreword perfectly captures my highest aspiration for myself.

Finally, to Jean: none of this is possible without your love, belief, patience, and endurance (especially with me!). Every day I become more grateful for you and the immortal diamond of friend and partner you are.

# NOTES

## Prologue

1. Doha Madani, "2 Mass Shootings in Less than a Day Leave at Least 29 Dead and 53 Injured," NBC News, August 5, 2019, https://www .nbcnews.com/news/us-news/2-mass-shootings-u-s-leave-least -29-dead-53-n1039066.

## Chapter 1: We Need to Remember

1. The story of the Roman concrete was inspired by Nicholas Christakis's excellent book, *Blueprint: The Evolutionary Origins of a Good Society* (New York: Little, Brown Spark, 2019).
2. Cigna Corporation, "2018 Cigna U.S. Loneliness Index," *American Journal of Health Promotion* (May 2018): https://www.cigna.com/assets /docs/newsroom/loneliness-survey-2018-full-report.pdf.
3. "Millennials Top Obesity Chart before Reaching Middle Age," Cancer Research UK, February 26, 2018, https://www.cancerresearchuk.org /about-us/cancer-news/press-release/2018-02-26-millennials-top -obesity-chart-before-reaching-middle-age; NHS Digital, "Health Survey for England, Trend Tables 2015," Gov.uk, December 14, 2016, https://www.gov.uk/government/statistics/health-survey-for-england -trend-tables-health-survey-for-england-trend-tables-2015.
4. Quoted in R. Morgan Griffin, "Obesity Epidemic 'Astronomical,'" WebMD, 2002, https://www.webmd.com/diet/obesity/features /obesity-epidemic-astronomical#1.
5. Quoted in Griffin, "Obesity Epidemic 'Astronomical.'"
6. David Harsanyi, "Millennials Are the Most Prosperous Generation That's Ever Lived," *Federalist*, March 22, 2019, https:// thefederalist.com/2019/03/22/stop-whining-millennials-youre -prosperous-generation-thats-ever-lived/.
7. "Understanding the Epidemic," Centers for Disease Control and

Prevention, December 19, 2018, https://www.cdc.gov/drugoverdose
/epidemic/index.html.

8. "Excessive Alcohol Use," Centers for Disease Control and Prevention,
June 26, 2019, https://www.cdc.gov/chronicdisease/resources/publications
/factsheets/alcohol.htm; "Alcohol Use," Centers for Disease Control and
Prevention, January 20, 2017, https://www.cdc.gov/nchs/fastats/alcohol.
htm; Hohenzollern, "Deaths of Despair: Modern America's Existential
Crisis," *Palace Intrigue*, September 6, 2019, https://palaceintrigueblog
.com/2019/09/06/deaths-of-despair-modern-americas-existential-crisis/;
Mike Allen, "One Big Thing: America Breaks a Terrible Trend," Axios PM,
January 30, 2020, https://www.axios.com/newsletters/axios-pm-1e42d590
-0db3-4317-b641-8e2ffb1053a6.html; Brittany Shoot, "Alcohol-Related
Deaths Are on the Rise, and Women Are Drinking More Alcohol than
Ever," *Fortune*, November 20, 2018, https://fortune.com/2018/11/20
/alcohol-related-deaths-drinking-women-mortality-rate/; "Long-Term
Trends in Deaths of Despair," United States Joint Economic Committee,
September 5, 2019, https://www.jec.senate.gov/public/index.cfm/republicans
/analysis?ID=B29A7E54-0E13-4C4D-83AA-6A49105F0F43.

9. Deborah M. Stone et al., "Vital Signs: Trends in State Suicide
Rates—United States, 1999–2016 and Circumstances Contributing to
Suicide—27 States, 2015," *Morbidity and Mortality Weekly Report* 67, no. 22
(June 8, 2018): 617–24, http://dx.doi.org/10.15585/mmwr.mm6722a1.

10. "Suicide," National Institute of Mental Health, US Department of
Health and Human Services, https://www.nimh.nih.gov/health
/statistics/suicide.shtml.

11. John Bacon, "'We Are Losing Too Many Americans': Suicides, Drug
Overdoses Rise as US Life Expectancy Drops," *USA Today*, November
29, 2018, https://www.usatoday.com/story/news/2018/11/29/us-life
-expectancy-suicide-50-year-peak-and-drugs-cause-death/2146829002/.

12. Dr. Edith Bracho-Sanchez, "Number of Children Going to ER with
Suicidal Thoughts, Attempts Doubles," CNN, April 8, 2019, https://www
.cnn.com/2019/04/08/health/child-teen-suicide-er-study/index.html.

13. Erin Duffin, "U.S. College Enrollment Statistics 1965–2028," Statista,
March 13, 2020, https://www.statista.com/statistics/183995/us-college
-enrollment-and-projections-in-public-and-private-institutions/.

14. Kasia Kovacs, "More People Enroll in College Even with Rising
Price Tag, Report Finds," Inside Higher Ed, September 22, 2016,

https://www.insidehighered.com/news/2016/09/22/more-people
-enroll-college-even-rising-price-tag-report-finds.

15. Clive Thompson, "Clive Thompson on How More Info Leads to Less Knowledge," *WIRED*, January 19, 2009, https://www.wired .com/2009/01/st-thompson-14/.

16. Alexa Lardieri, "Study: People Are Getting Dumber," *U.S. News & World Report*, June 14, 2018, https://www.usnews.com/news/national -news/articles/2018-06-14/study-people-are-getting-dumber.

17. Hosea 4:6

18. Marie D. Jackson et al., "Phillipsite and Al-Tobermorite Mineral Cements Produced through Low-Temperature Water-Rock Reactions in Roman Marine Concrete," *American Mineralogist* 102, no. 7 (2017): 1435–50, https://doi.org/10.2138/am-2017-5993ccby.

19. University of Utah, "New Studies of Ancient Concrete Could Teach Us to Do as the Romans Did," Phys.org, July 3, 2017, https://phys.org /news/2017-07-ancient-concrete-romans.html.

## Chapter 2: You Have a Purpose

1. Declaration of Independence, United States of America, https://www .archives.gov/founding-docs/declaration-transcript.

2. Matthew 5:5

3. John Locke, "Concerning Human Understanding", Essay, 1690. I will spare you the additional brain damage, but Locke went a lot deeper into that idea, clarifying that this "true happiness" often means not satisfying our desires in favor of virtue, or what we are truly meant to do—our purpose.

4. John Stuart Mill, *Utilitarianism*, 1863. The prominent twentieth-century writer Huxley starkly stated, "The right to the pursuit of happiness is nothing else than the right to disillusionment phrased in another way" (Aldous Huxley, "Tomorrow and Tomorrow and Tomorrow," 1956).

5. Ruth Whippman, *America the Anxious: Why Our Search for Happiness Is Driving Us Crazy and How to Find It for Real* (New York: St. Martin's, 2016), 9.

6. Hannah Fingerhut, "Already-Low Voter Satisfaction with Choice of Candidates Falls Even Further," Pew Research Center, September 12, 2016, https://www.pewresearch.org/fact-tank/2016/09/12/already-low -voter-satisfaction-with-choice-of-candidates-falls-even-further/.

7. https://oqfarm.org

8. Saint Irenaeus of Lyons, *Against Heresies*, IV.20.7: 649: "Gloria enim Dei ita autem hominis visio Dei."

9. Genesis 1:27

10. Luke Girgis, "Chris Pratt: 'People Will Tell You That You Are Perfect Just the Way You Are, You Are Not!'" *Brag*, June 26, 2018, https://thebrag.com/chris-pratt-people-will-tell-you-that-you-are-perfect-just-way-you-are-you-are-not/.

11. Richard Rohr, *Immortal Diamond: The Search for Our True Self* (San Francisco: Jossey Bass, 2013), 57.

12. Rick Warren, *The Purpose Driven Life: What on Earth Am I Here For?* (Grand Rapids: Zondervan, 2012), 24, 194.

13. Quoted in Hugh S. Moorhead, *The Meaning of Life* (Chicago: Chicago Review Press, 1988), 164.

14. Warren, *The Purpose Driven Life*, 21, 22.

15. Alcoholics Anonymous, *Understanding Anonymity* (New York: Alcoholics Anonymous World Services, Inc., 2018), 14.

16. *Alcoholics Anonymous: The Big Book*, 4th ed. (New York: Alcoholics Anonymous World Services, Inc., 2001), 306.

17. University College London, "Sense of Meaning and Purpose in Life Linked to Longer Lifespan," November 6, 2014, ScienceDaily, https://www.sciencedaily.com/releases/2014/11/141106211618.htm.

18. Patrick L. Hill and Nicholas A. Turiano, "Purpose in Life as a Predictor of Mortality across Adulthood," *Psychological Science* 25, no. 7 (July 2014): 1482–86, https://doi.org/10.1177/0956797614531799.

19. Hill and Turiano, "Purpose in Life."

20. Naomi I. Eisenberger et al., "Inflammation and Social Experience: An Inflammatory Challenge Induces Feelings of Social Disconnection in Addition to Depressed Mood," *Brain, Behavior, and Immunity* 24, no. 4 (May 2010): 558–63, https://doi.org/10.1016/j.bbi.2009.12.009; Edward Bullmore, *The Inflamed Mind: A Radical New Approach to Depression* (New York: Picador, 2018).

21. The Emerging Risk Factors Collaboration, "C-Reactive Protein Concentration and Risk of Coronary Heart Disease, Stroke, and Mortality: An Individual Participant Meta-Analysis," *Lancet* 375, no. 9709 (January 9, 2010): 132–40, https://doi.org/10.1016/S0140-6736(09)61717-7.

22. Barbara L. Fredrickson et al., "Psychological Well-Being and the

Human Conserved Transcriptional Response to Adversity," *PLOS One* 10, no. 3, e0121839 (March 26, 2015), https://doi.org/10.1371/journal .pone.0121839; Barbara L. Fredrickson et al., "A Functional Genomic Perspective on Human Well-Being," *Proceedings of the National Academy of Sciences of the United States of America* 110, no. 33 (August 13, 2013): 13684–89, https://doi.org/10.1073/pnas.1305419110.

23. Iris B. Mauss et al., "Can Seeking Happiness Make People Unhappy? Paradoxical Effects of Valuing Happiness," *Emotion* 11, no. 4 (August 2011): 807, https://www.ncbi.nlm.nih.gov/pmc/articles/PMC3160511/; Iris B. Mauss et al., "The Pursuit of Happiness Can Be Lonely," *Emotion* 12, no. 5 (2012): 908; Amy L. Gentzler et al., "Valuing Happiness in Youth: Associations with Depressive Symptoms and Well-Being," *Journal of Applied Developmental Psychology* 62 (May–June 2019): 220–30, https:// www.sciencedirect.com/science/article/pii/S019339731730374X.

24. Tyler J. VanderWeele, "Religious Upbringing and Adolescence," Institute for Family Studies, September 18, 2018, https://ifstudies.org/blog /religious-upbringing-and-adolescence.

## Chapter 3: You Long For Renewal

1. Sheena S. Iyengar and Mark R. Lepper, "When Choice Is Demotivating: Can One Desire Too Much of a Good Thing?" *Journal of Personality and Social Psychology* 79, no. 6 (2000): 995–1006, https://doi.org /10.1037/0022-3514.79.6.995.

2. Iyengar and Lepper, "When Choice Is Demotivating."

3. Barry Schwartz, "Transcript of 'The Paradox of Choice,'" July 2005, TED, https://www.ted.com/talks/barry_schwartz_the_paradox _of_choice/transcript?language=en.

4. Shwartz, "Transcript of 'The Paradox of Choice.'"

5. Barry Schwartz, "More Isn't Always Better," *Harvard Business Review* (June 2006), https://hbr.org/2006/06/more-isnt-always-better.

6. Schwartz, "Transcript of 'The Paradox of Choice.'"

7. Schwartz, "Transcript of 'The Paradox of Choice.'"

8. Jeff White, "Tony Bennett Declined a Raise. Then He and His Wife Pledged $500k to Career Program," University of Virginia, September 15, 2019, https://news.virginia.edu/content/tony-bennett-declined-raise -then-he-and-his-wife-pledged-500k-career-program.

9. White, "Tony Bennett Declined a Raise."

10. Thomas Franck, "Federal Deficit Increases 26% to $984 Billion for Fiscal 2019, Highest in 7 Years." CNBC, October 25, 2019, https://www.cnbc.com/2019/10/25/federal-deficit-increases-26percent-to-984-billion-for-fiscal-2019.html.

11. "How Income Volatility Interacts with American Families' Financial Security," PEW Charitable Trusts, March 9, 2017, https://www.pewtrusts.org/en/research-and-analysis/issue-briefs/2017/03/how-income-volatility-interacts-with-american-families-financial-security.

12. "Stress in America: Paying with Our Health," American Psychological Association, February 4, 2015, https://www.apa.org/news/press/releases/stress/2014/stress-report.pdf.

13. Laura M. Argys, Andrew I. Friedson, and M. Melinda Pitts, "Killer Debt: The Impact of Debt on Mortality," Federal Reserve Bank of Atlanta, November 2016, https://www.frbatlanta.org/-/media/documents/research/publications/wp/2016/14-killer-debt-the-impact-of-debt-on-mortality-2017-04-10.pdf.

14. John Gathergood, "Debt and Depression: Causal Links and Social Norm Effects," *The Economic Journal* 122, no. 563 (January 9, 2012): 1094–1114, https://doi.org/10.1111/j.1468-0297.2012.02519.x.

15. Matthew 6:25–26, 28–30 ESV

16. Ecclesiastes 2:17–18

17. Daniel Schorn, "Transcript: Tom Brady, Part 3." CBS News, November 4, 2005, https://www.cbsnews.com/news/transcript-tom-brady-part-3/.

18. Jack Maloney, "NBA Commissioner Adam Silver on Mental Health of League: 'A Lot of Players Are Unhappy,'" CBS Sports, March 4, 2019, https://www.cbssports.com/nba/news/nba-commissioner-adam-silver-on-mental-health-of-league-a-lot-of-players-are-unhappy/; "Silver Talks Player Anxiety, Potential NBA Changes," ESPN, March 1, 2019, https://www.espn.com/nba/story/_/id/26114198/silver-talks-player-anxiety-potential-nba-changes/.

19. "Search Our Salary Database of California State Workers," *Sacramento Bee*, April 16, 2019, https://www.sacbee.com/news/databases/state-pay/article229468549.html.

20. "Search Our Salary Database of California State Workers," *Sacramento Bee*, April 16, 2019, https://www.sacbee.com/news/databases/state-pay/article229468549.html.

21. Psalm 23:1

22. Psalm 23:2
23. Psalm 13
24. Beatrice Lumpkin, "Needed: A Shorter Work Week," *People's World*, December 17, 2018, https://www.peoplesworld.org/article/needed -a-shorter-work-week/.
25. Lumpkin, "Needed."
26. Lumpkin, "Needed."
27. "State of American Vacation 2018," US Travel Association, May 8, 2018, https://www.ustravel.org/research/state-american-vacation-2018.
28. Rober W. Dunne, *Tao Te Ching by Lao Tzu* (United States: AuthorHouse, 2008), 35.
29. Ahmed S. BaHammam, "Sleep from an Islamic Perspective," *Annals of Thoracic Medicine* 6, no. 4 (2011): 187–92, https://doi.org/10.4103/1817 -1737.84771.
30. Josef Pieper, *Leisure: The Basis of Culture* (San Francisco: Ignatius, 2009).
31. Jeffrey M. Jones, "In U.S., 40% Get Less Than Recommended Amount of Sleep," Gallup, December 19, 2013, https://news.gallup.com/poll /166553/less-recommended-amount-sleep.aspx.x.
32. Neil Howe, "America the Sleep-Deprived," *Forbes*, August 18, 2017, https://www.forbes.com/sites/neilhowe/2017/08/18/america -the-sleep-deprived/#b0cfe301a385.
33. Exodus 20:8
34. Nathaniel Lee, "Warren Buffett Lives in a Modest House That's Worth .001% of His Total Wealth—Here's What It Looks Like," *Business Insider*, December 4, 2017, https://www.businessinsider.com/warren -buffett-modest-home-bought-31500-looks-2017-6.
35. Charles Passy, "For $6, a Chance to Beat Warren Buffett at His Own Game," MarketWatch, May 4, 2015, https://www.marketwatch.com /story/you-could-play-bridge-with-warren-buffett-at-his-bridge-club -but-itll-cost-you-2015-05-01.
36. Marcel Schwantes, "Warren Buffett Says This One Simple Habit Separates Successful People from Everyone Else." Inc., January 18, 2018, https://www.inc.com/marcel-schwantes/warren-buffett-says-this-is-1 -simple-habit-that-separates-successful-people-from-everyone-else.html.

## Chapter 4: You Will Face Adversity

1. Matt Fitzgerald, *How Bad Do You Want It? Mastering the Psychology of Mind over Muscle* (Boulder: VeloPress, 2016), Kindle edition, chapter 5.
2. Fitzgerald, *How Bad Do You Want It?*, chapter 5.
3. Marcus Aurelius, *Meditations: A New Translation* (New York: Random House, 2002), 60.
4. Aurelius, *Meditations: A New Translation*.
5. Epictetus puts it far more eloquently than I do in his ancient books *Discourses* and *The Enchiridion*; Epictetus, *Discourses of Epictetus*, trans. George Long (New York: D. Appleton and Company, 1904); Epictetus, *The Enchiridion*, trans. Elizabeth Carter, Internet Classics Archive, http://classics.mit.edu/Epictetus/epicench.html.
6. Nassim Nicholas Taleb, *Antifragile: Things That Gain from Disorder* (New York: Random House, 2016), 156.
7. Hebrews 13:5
8. Viktor E. Frankl, *Man's Search for Meaning* (Boston: Beacon, 2006), 66.
9. Brené Brown, *Rising Strong: How the Ability to Reset Transforms the Way We Live, Love, Parent, and Lead* (New York: Random House, 2015), xxviii.
10. Rosa Parks with James Haskins, *Rosa Parks: My Story* (New York: Scholastic, 1992), 116.
11. Rosa Parks and Gregory J. Reed, *Quiet Strength: The Faith, the Hope, and the Heart of a Woman Who Changed a Nation* (Grand Rapids: Zondervan, 1994), 17.
12. Wim Hof, in the foreword to Scott Carney's *What Doesn't Kill Us: How Freezing Water, Extreme Altitude, and Environmental Conditioning Will Renew Our Lost Evolutionary Strength* (New York: Rodale, 2017), x.
13. Carney, *What Doesn't Kill Us*, 18.
14. Carney, *What Doesn't Kill Us*, 39–40.
15. Sergio R. Angeles, "Author Scott Carney Looks at the Power behind What Doesn't Kill Us in September 25 Library Program," *Longmont Observer*, September 14, 2017, https://longmontobserver.org/lifestyle chapter 5/author-scott-carney-looks-power-behind-doesnt-kill-us chapter 5-september-25-library-program/.
16. Dan P. McAdams and Jen Guo, "Narrating the Generative Life," *Psychological Science* 26, no. 4 (May 2015): 475–83, https://doi.org/10.1177/0956797614568318.
17. McAdams and Guo, "Narrating the Generative Life," 475.

18. The full quote is "The arc of the moral universe is long, but it bends toward justice." In Theodore Parker, *Ten Sermons on Religion* (London: Crosby, Nichols, and Company, 1853), 78.

19. Will Durant and Ariel Durant, *The Lessons of History* (New York: Simon & Schuster, 2010), 91.

20. Kyle Dickman, "The Future of Disaster Relief Isn't the Red Cross," *Outside*, August 25, 2016, https://www.outsideonline.com/2106556 /team-rubicon-takes-red-cross.

21. "Jake Wood Accepts Pat Tillman Award for Service—ESPN Video," ESPN, accessed January 21, 2020, https://www.espn.com/video/clip /_/id/24133915.

## Chapter 5: You Need People

1. Matthew D. Lieberman, *Social: Why Our Brains Are Wired to Connect* (Oxford: Oxford University Press, 2013), 9.

2. Lieberman, *Social*, 126.

3. Martin Buber, *I and Thou* (London: A&C Black, 2004), 82.

4. Jim Vandehei, "Jim Vandehei Transcript," interview by Bill Kristol, *Conversations with Bill Kristol*, September 11, 2019, https:// conversationswithbillkristol.org/transcript/jim-vandehei-transcript/.

5. Michael Winnick, "Putting a Finger on Our Phone Obsession: Mobile Touches: A Study on How Humans Use Technology," DScout, June 16, 2016, https://blog.dscout.com/mobile-touches.

6. Shalini Misra et al., "The iPhone Effect: The Quality of In-Person Social Interactions in the Presence of Mobile Devices," *Environment and Behavior* 48, no. 2 (July 1, 2014): 275–98, https://journals.sagepub.com/doi/abs /10.1177/0013916514539755.

7. "Siberian Lake Frequented for Instagram Photo Shoots Is Actually Full of Toxic Waste," *USA Today*, July 14, 2019, https://www.usatoday.com /story/travel/news/2019/07/14/instagram-photo-haven-siberian-lake -actually-full-toxic-waste/1728370001/.

8. Julie Jargon, "The Dark Side of Discord, Your Teen's Favorite Chat App," *Wall Street Journal*, June 11, 2019, https://www.wsj.com/articles /discord-where-teens-rule-and-parents-fear-to-tread-11560245402.

9. Jargon, "Dark Side of Discord."

10. Avi Selk, "YouTuber Etika Found Dead in East River, Following a Series of Erratic Videos and Police Confrontations," *Washington Post*,

June 26, 2019, https://www.washingtonpost.com/lifestyle/2019/06/25
/youtuber-etika-found-dead-east-river-following-series-erratic-videos
-police-confrontations/.

11. Selk, "YouTuber Etika Found Dead."
12. Dale Carnegie, *How to Win Friends and Influence People* (New York: Simon & Schuster, 1981), xvi.
13. Dale Carnegie and Brent Cole, *How to Win Friends and Influence People in the Digital Age* (New York: Simon & Schuster, 2011), ix.
14. Carnegie and Cole, *How to Win Friends and Influence People in the Digital Age*, xxi.
15. Carol Kinsey Goman, "Has Technology Killed Face-to-Face Communication?" *Forbes*, November 14, 2018, https://www.forbes.com/sites/carolkinseygoman/2018/11/14/has-technology-killed-face-to-face-communication/#32deba90a8cc.
16. Albert Mehrabian, *Silent Messages: Implicit Communication of Emotions and Attitudes* (Belmont, CA: Wadsworth, 1971), 44.
17. Justin Kruger et al., "Egocentrism over E-mail: Can We Communicate as Well as We Think?" *Journal of Personality and Social Psychology* 89, no. 6 (December 2005): 925–36, https://doi.org/10.1037/0022-3514.89.6.925.f.
18. A 2017 study by Vanessa Bohns of Cornell University and Mahdi Roghanizad of Western University showed that face-to-face communication is thirty-four times more effective than an email. And yet the study participants believed their email communication would be *more* effective than their in-person communication (they were asking people to donate money). Of the results, Bohns wrote, "Despite the reach of email, asking in-person is the significantly more effective approach; you need to ask six people in person to equal the power of a 200-recipient email blast. Still, most people tend to think the email ask will be more effective." M. Mahdi Roghanizad and Vanessa K. Bohns, "Ask in Person: You're Less Persuasive Than You Think over Email," *Journal of Experimental Social Psychology* 69 (March 2017): 223–26, https://doi.org/10.1016/j.jesp.2016.10.002.
19. Lauren E. Sherman, Minas Michikyan, and Patricia M. Greenfield, "The Effects of Text, Audio, Video, and In-Person Communication on Bonding among Friends," *Cyberpsychology: Journal of Psychosocial Research on Cyberspace* 7, no. 2, article 3 (2013), http://dx.doi.org/10.5817/CP2013-2-3.

20. Allana Akhtar, "Bill Gates and Steve Jobs Raised Their Kids Tech-Free—and It Should've Been a Red Flag," *Business Insider,* September 30, 2019, https://www.businessinsider.com/screen-time -limits-bill-gates-steve-jobs-red-flag-2017-10.

21. Akhtar, "Bill Gates."

22. Akhtar, "Bill Gates."

23. Quoted in "How to Get Better at Video Games," Twofivesix, September 10, 2019, https://twofivesix.co/how-to-get-better-at-video-games/.

24. Carmine Gallo, "Texas Tech's Coach Taught His Team a Lost Art—and It Sent Them to the NCAA Final Four," Inc., April 4, 2019, https:// www.inc.com/carmine-gallo/texas-techs-coach-taught-his-team-a-lost -art-and-it-sent-them-to-ncaa-final-four.html.

25. Gallo, "Texas Tech's Coach."

26. Sherry Turkle, *Reclaiming Conversation: The Power of Talk in a Digital Age* (New York: Penguin, 2016), 3.

27. Robert Frost, "A Time to Talk," in *The Poetry of Robert Frost: The Collected Poems,* ed. Edward Connery Lathem (New York: Henry Holt and Company, 1969), 124.

28. "2020 Nissan Altima TV Commercial, 'Text Answering' [T1]." iSpot.tv, 2019, https://www.ispot.tv/ad/ZfiP/2020-nissan-altima -text-answering-t1.

## Chapter 6: You Are Not Alone

1. "Criminal Justice Facts," The Sentencing Project, accessed January 21, 2020, https://www.sentencingproject.org/criminal-justice-facts/.

2. "Criminal Justice Fact Sheet," NAACP, n.d, https://www.naacp.org /criminal-justice-fact-sheet/.

3. Andrew Sullivan, "The Poison We Pick," *Intelligencer,* February 19, 2018, https://nymag.com/intelligencer/2018/02/americas-opioid-epidemic.html.

4. Alix Spiegel, "What Vietnam Taught Us about Breaking Bad Habits," NPR, January 2, 2012, https://www.npr.org/sections /health-shots/2012/01/02/144431794/what-vietnam-taught-us-about -breaking-bad-habits.

5. Spiegel, "What Vietnam Taught Us."

6. Bruce K. Alexander et al., "Effect of Early and Later Colony Housing on Oral Ingestion of Morphine in Rats," *Pharmacology Biochemistry and Behavior* 15, no. 4 (1981): 571–76, https://doi.org/10.1016/0091 -3057(81)90211-2.

7. Marco Venniro et al., "Volitional Social Interaction Prevents Drug Addiction in Rat Models," *Nature Neuroscience* 21, no. 11 (2018): 1520–29, https://doi.org/10.1038/s41593-018-0246-6.

8. Sam Quinones, *Dreamland: The True Tale of America's Opiate Epidemic* (New York: Bloomsbury, 2015), 8.

9. Alexis de Tocqueville, *Democracy in America* (1835; New York: Penguin, 2003), 596.

10. Timothy P. Carney, *Alienated America: Why Some Places Thrive While Others Collapse* (New York: HarperCollins, 2019).

11. Peter Beinart, "Breaking Faith," *Atlantic*, April 15, 2017, https://www.theatlantic.com/magazine/archive/2017/04/breaking-faith/517785/.

12. Carroll Doherty, Jocelyn Kiley, and Bridget Johnson, "The Public, the Political System and American Democracy," Pew Research Center, April 26, 2018, http://assets.pewresearch.org/wp-content/uploads/sites/5/2018/04/26140617/4-26-2018-Democracy-release.pdf.

13. Jamie Ducharme, "Suicide Rates Are the Highest They've Been Since WWII," *Time*, June 20, 2019, https://time.com/5609124/us-suicide-rate-increase/; Sabrina Tavernise, "Young Adolescents as Likely to Die from Suicide as from Traffic Accidents," *New York Times*, November 3, 2016, https://www.nytimes.com/2016/11/04/health/suicide-adolescents-traffic-deaths.html.

14. Julianne Holt-Lunstad, Timothy B. Smith, and J. Bradley Layton, "Social Relationships and Mortality Risk: A Meta-Analytic Review," *PLOS Medicine* 7, no. 7 (July 2010): e1000316, https://www.ncbi.nlm.nih.gov/pmc/articles/PMC2910600/; Sarah Schmalbruch, "10 Ways Loneliness Can Affect Your Health—Physically and Mentally," *Insider*, November 13, 2018, https://www.insider.com/effects-loneliness-health-2018-6#loneliness-can-lead-to-depression-2.

15. R. Lund, C. J. Nilsson, and K. Avlund, "Can the Higher Risk of Disability Onset among Older People Who Live Alone Be Alleviated by Strong Social Relations? A Longitudinal Study of Non-disabled Men and Women," *Age and Ageing* 39, no. 3 (May 2010): 319–326, http://www.ncbi.nlm.nih.gov/pubmed/20208073.

16. J. T. Cacioppo et al., "Loneliness as a Specific Risk Factor for Depressive Symptoms: Cross-Sectional and Longitudinal Analyses," *Psychology and Aging* 21, no. 1 (March 2006): 140–51, http://www.ncbi.nlm.nih.gov/pubmed/16594799.

17. B. D. James et al., "Late-Life Social Activity and Cognitive Decline in

Old Age," *Journal of the International Neuropsychological Society* 17, no. 6 (November 2011): 998–1005, http://www.ncbi.nlm.nih.gov/pubmed /22040898.

18. Henry O'Connell et al., "Recent Developments: Suicide in Older People," *British Medical Journal* 329, no. 7471 (October 16, 2004): 895–99, https://www.ncbi.nlm.nih.gov/pmc/articles/PMC523116/.

19. Tjalling Jan Holwerda et al., "Research Paper: Feelings of Loneliness, but Not Social Isolation, Predict Dementia Onset: Results from the Amsterdam Study of the Elderly (AMSTEL)," *Journal of Neurology, Neurosurgery and Psychiatry* 85 (2014): 135–42, http://jnnp.bmj.com /content/early/2012/11/06/jnnp-2012-302755.

20. Holt-Lunstad, Smith , and Layton, "Social Relationships and Mortality Risk: A Meta-Analytic Review"; Justin Worland, "Why Loneliness May Be the Next Big Public-Health Issue," *Time*, March 18, 2015.

21. Cigna Corporation, "2018 Cigna U.S. Loneliness Index," *American Journal of Health Promotion*, May 2018, https://www.cigna.com/assets /docs/newsroom/loneliness-survey-2018-full-report.pdf.

22. Sullivan, "Poison We Pick."

23. Dave Armstrong, "Mother Teresa on Love and Theology," Biblical Evidence for Catholicism, Patheos, September 5, 2016, https://www .patheos.com/blogs/davearmstrong/2016/09/mother-teresa-on-love -theology.html/2.

24. Robert Putnam, *Bowling Alone: The Collapse and Revival of American Community* (New York: Simon & Schuster, 2001), 289.

25. A. Pratibha, "The Stockdale Paradox," *HuffPost*, February 5, 2017, https://www.huffpost.com/entry/the-stockdale-paradox _b_5897ca82e4b02bbb1816bc38.

26. "The Stockdale Paradox: Audio Transcript," Jim Collins, 2017, https:// www.jimcollins.com/media_topics/TheStockdaleParadox.html.

27. James C. Collins, *Good to Great: Why Some Companies Make the Leap . . . and Others Don't* (New York: Random House Business, 2001), 13.

28. Matthew D. Lieberman, *Social: Why Our Brains Are Wired to Connect* (New York: Crown, 2013), 299.

29. Ephesians 5:13

30. Andy Crouch, *The Tech-Wise Family: Everyday Steps for Putting Technology in Its Proper Place* (Grand Rapids: Baker, 2017), 42.

31. Sullivan, "Poison We Pick."

## Chapter 7: We Are More Alike Than Different

1. "Can I Play That?" *Saturday Night Live*, NBC Universal Media, March 9, 2019, https://www.nbc.com/saturday-night-live/video/can-i -play-that/3920139.

2. "Can I Play That?" *Saturday Night Live*.

3. Katherine Timpf, "Study: 80 Percent of People Think 'Political Correctness Is a Problem in Our Country,'" *National Review*, October 12, 2018, https://www.nationalreview.com/2018/10/political -correctness-problem-according-to-80-percent-of-people/.

4. Katherine Timpf, "Professor: Small Chairs in Preschools Are Sexist, 'Problematic,' and 'Disempowering,'" *National Review*, January 22, 2018, https://www.nationalreview.com/2018/01/preschoolers -small-chairs-sexist-problematic-disempowering/.

5. Jonah Goldberg, *Suicide of the West: How the Rebirth of Tribalism, Populism, Nationalism, and Identity Politics Is Destroying American Democracy* (New York: Crown, 2019), 59.

6. Drew Harwell, "Faked Pelosi Videos, Slowed to Make Her Appear Drunk, Spread across Social Media," *Washington Post*, May 24, 2019, https://www.washingtonpost.com/technology/2019/05/23/faked-pelosi -videos-slowed-make-her-appear-drunk-spread-across-social-media/.

7. Quoted in Alexi, McCammond, "Why Instagram Could Be a 2020 Disinformation Weapon," Axios, September 9, 2019, https://www.axios .com/new-fake-news-worry-for-instagram-64583147-3977-4b64-a0e8 -a191872f60a4.html.

8. Emily Stewart, "Facebook Has Taken Down Billions of Fake Accounts, but the Problem Is Still Getting Worse," Vox, May 23, 2019, https://www.vox.com/recode/2019/5/23/18637596/facebook -fake-accounts-transparency-mark-zuckerberg-report.

9. Stefan Wojcik et al., "Twitter Bots: An Analysis of the Links Automated Accounts Share," Pew Research Center, April 9, 2018, https://www .pewresearch.org/internet/2018/04/09/bots-in-the-twittersphere/.

10. Garry Kasparov (@Kasparov63), "The point of modern propaganda isn't only to misinform or push an agenda. It is to exhaust your critical thinking, to annihilate truth," Twitter, December 13, 2016, https:// twitter.com/kasparov63/status/808750564284702720?lang=en.

11. Peter Pomerantsev, *This Is Not Propaganda: Adventures in the War Against Reality* (London: Faber & Faber, 2019); see also Sabrina Tavernise and

Aidan Gardiner, "'No One Believes Anything': Voters Worn Out by a Fog of Political News," *New York Times*, November 18, 2019, https://www.nytimes.com/2019/11/18/us/polls-media-fake-news.html.

12. Hannah Arendt, "Truth and Politics," *New Yorker*, February 25, 1967, 78.

13. Scott Rosenberg and David Nather, "The Misinformation Age," Axios, September 12, 2019, https://www.axios.com/the-misinformation-age -0f044c65-7cd8-4194-a49e-110e90184cd5.html.

14. Lee Rainie, Scott Keeter, and Andrew Perrin, "Trust and Distrust in America," Pew Research Center, July 22, 2019, https://www .people-press.org/2019/07/22/trust-and-distrust-in-america/?utm _source=newsletter&utm_medium=email&utm_campaign=newsletter _axiosam&stream=top.

15. Carroll Doherty and Jocelyn Kiley, "Partisanship and Political Animosity in America: 6 Key Facts," Pew Research Center, June 22, 2016, https://www.pewresearch.org/fact-tank/2016/06/22/key-facts-partisanship/.

16. Dexter Filkins, "James Mattis, a Warrior in Washington," *New Yorker*, May 22, 2017, https://www.newyorker.com/magazine/2017/05/29 /james-mattis-a-warrior-in-washington.

17. Stephen Hawkins et al., "Hidden Tribes: A Study of America's Polarized Landscape," More in Common, 2018, 4, https://static1.squarespace .com/static/5a70a7c3010027736a22740f/t/5bbcea6b7817f7bf73 42b718/1539107467397/hidden_tribes_report-2.pdf.

18. Hawkins et al., "Hidden Tribes," 15.

19. Stephen R. Covey, *The 7 Habits of Highly Effective People: Powerful Lessons in Personal Change* (New York: Simon & Schuster, 2004), 237.

20. "Peace Prayer of Saint Francis," Loyola Press, March 12, 2018, https://www.loyolapress.com/our-catholic-faith/prayer/traditional -catholic-prayers/saints-prayers/peace-prayer-of-saint-francis.

21. Jonathan Haidt, *The Righteous Mind: Why Good People Are Divided by Politics and Religion* (New York: Pantheon, 2012), 318.

22. Arthur Schopenhauer, *Counsels and Maxims*, trans. T. Bailey Saunders (1851), vol. 2, chap. 24, 324.

23. Arthur C. Brooks, *Love Your Enemies: How Decent People Can Save America from the Culture of Contempt* (New York: HarperCollins, 2019), 64.

24. Brooks, *Love Your Enemies*, 22.

25. John Gottman and Nan Silver, *Why Marriages Succeed or Fail: And How You Can Make Yours Last* (London: A&C Black, 2012), 79–80.

26. Andrew Ferguson, "Can Marriage Counseling Save America?" *Atlantic*, November 12, 2019, https://www.theatlantic.com/magazine /archive/2019/12/better-angels-can-this-union-be-saved/600775/.

27. LaTesha Harris, "Ellen DeGeneres Defends George W. Bush Friendship: 'We're All Different,'" *Variety*, October 8, 2019, https:// variety.com/2019/tv/news/ellen-degeneres-defends-george-w-bush -friendship-1203363515/.

28. Harris, "Ellen DeGeneres Defends George W. Bush."

29. Naomi LaChance, "Ellen Staunchly Defends Her Nauseating Friendship with George W. Bush," Splinter, October 8, 2019, https://splinternews.com/ellen-staunchly-defends-her-nauseating -friendship-with-1838864797.

30. Ashley Collman, "Michelle Obama Defends Ellen DeGeneres after She Was Ridiculed for Her Friendship with George W. Bush: 'Our Values Are the Same,'" *Business Insider*, December 10, 2019, https://www .businessinsider.com/michelle-obama-defend-ellen-degeneres-friendship -george-w-bush-2019-12.

31. Anthony G. Greenwald, Debbie E. McGhee, and Jordan L. K. Schwartz, "Measuring Individual Difference in Implicit Cognition: The Implicit Association Test," *Journal of Personality and Social Psychology* 74, no. 6 (1998): 1464–80, https://faculty.washington.edu/agg/pdf/Gwald_McGh _Schw_JPSP_1998.OCR.pdf.

32. Anthony G. Greenwald and Mahzarin R. Banaji, "Implicit Social Cognition: Attitudes, Self-Esteem, and Stereotypes," *Psychological Review* 102, no. 1 (1995): 6–8, http://www.people.fas.harvard.edu/~banaji /research/publications/articles/1995_Greenwald_PR.pdf."

33. Malcolm Gladwell, *Blink: The Power of Thinking without Thinking* (New York: Back Bay, 2005), 84.

34. Michele Sullivan, *Looking Up: How a Different Perspective Turns Obstacles into Advantages* (Nashville: HarperCollins Leadership, 2020), xvi.

35. Sullivan, *Looking Up*, 88.

## Chapter 8: I Am You Are We

1. Victoria McGrane, "In Shift, Teamsters Back Baker for Reelection," n.d. http://edition.pagesuite.com/popovers/article_popover.aspx?guid =6557b4d1-b24c-4464-8c99-9d57bd3f4c73.

2. A. H. Maslow, "A Theory of Human Motivation," *Psychological Review* 50, no. 4 (1943): 370–96, https://doi.org/10.1037/h0054346; Saul

Mcleod, "Maslow's Hierarchy of Needs," Simply Psychology, May 21, 2018, https://www.simplypsychology.org/maslow.html.

3. "Anthropologists and Interpreter on the Blackfoot (Siksika) Reserve, Alberta," Archives Society of Alberta, March 16, 2013, https://albertaonrecord.ca/is-glen-3802.

4. Cindy Blackstock, "The Emergency of the Breath of Life Theory," *Journal of Social Work Values and Ethics* 8, no. 1 (2011), https://jswve.org/download/2011-1/spr11-blackstock-Emergence-breath-of-life-theory.pdf.

5. Sarena Johnson, "The Blackfoot/Maslow Connection," SA Exchange, September 20, 2018, https://sa-exchange.ca/the-blackfoot-maslow-connection/.

6. Matthew 22:37–40

7. Revelation 7:9–10 NLT

8. Matthew 27:46

9. Luke 23:34

10. Matthew 18:22 NLT

11. Luke 6:27

12. Martin L. King, "Draft of Chapter IV, 'Love in Action,'" The Martin Luther King, Jr., Research and Education Institute, Stanford University, May 3, 2017, https://kinginstitute.stanford.edu/king-papers/documents/draft-chapter-iv-love-action.

13. King, "Draft of Chapter IV."

14. "I Forgive You," YouTube, October 2, 2019, https://www.youtube.com/watch?time_continue=11&v=vYsMlKCa9EQ&feature=emb_logo.

15. "I Forgive You," YouTube.

16. Ashley Killough and Madeline Holcombe, "Emotions Run High in and outside of Courtroom after Amber Guyger Sentenced to 10 Years for Botham Jean's Murder," CNN, October 3, 2019, https://www.cnn.com/2019/10/03/us/botham-jean-amber-guyger-trial-wrap/index.html.

17. Mitch Mitchell, "Botham Jean's Younger Brother Hugs Amber Guyger, Says He Forgives Her after Murder." *Fort Worth Star-Telegram*, October 2, 2019, https://www.star-telegram.com/news/local/crime/article235733587.html.

18. Mitchell, "Botham Jean's Younger Brother."

19. Kevin Aldridge, "Opinion: Brandt Jean Publicly Forgave His Brother's Killer. Was It Too Soon?" *Cincinnati Enquirer*, October 4, 2019, https://www.cincinnati.com/story/opinion/2019/10/04/opinion-brandt-jean-publicly-forgave-his-brothers-killer-too-soon/3856378002/.

## Chapter 9: Together We Will Awaken America

1. Thomas Jefferson, "Notes on the State of Virginia, Query XVII," 1781, 272.
2. United States Congress, Congressional Record: Proceedings and Debates of the United States Congress, US Government Printing Office, 2008, 1303.
3. A. Leon Higginbotham, *In the Matter of Color: Race and the American Legal Process* (New York: Oxford University Press, 1998), 384n55.
4. Abraham Lincoln, "Speech on the Dred Scott Decision," in *Abraham Lincoln: Speeches and Writings*, vol. 1 *1832–1858*, ed. Don E. Fehrenbacher (New York: The Library of America, 1989), ebook edition.
5. "'I Am Prepared to Die,'" Nelson Mandela Foundation, April 20, 2011, https://www.nelsonmandela.org/news/entry/i-am-prepared-to-die.
6. Congressional Volume 154, Number 17, February 4, 2008, 605, From the Congressional Record Online through the Government Publishing Office, https://www.govinfo.gov/content/pkg/CREC-2008-02-04 /html/CREC-2008-02-04-pt1-PgS603-2.htm.
7. Congressional Volume 154, 605.
8. "About Frederick Douglass," https://frederickdouglassinstitute.org /about-frederick-douglass/.
9. Drew Dickson, "Stay in the Game," Albert Bridge Capital, June 17, 2019, https://www.albertbridgecapital.com/post/stay-in-the-game.
10. Winston S. Churchill, *The Grand Alliance: The Second World War*, vol. 3 (Boston: Houghton Mifflin, 1977), 540.
11. *Inaugural Addresses of the Presidents of the United States* (Washington, DC: U.S. G.P.O.: for sale by the Supt. of Docs., U.S. G.P.O., 1989); Bartleby .com, 2001, https://www.bartleby.com/124/pres31.html.
12. "Second Inaugural Addresses of Abraham Lincoln," Avalon Project: Documents in Law, History and Diplomacy, Yale University Law School, n.d., https://avalon.law.yale.edu/19th_century/lincoln2.asp.

## Epilogue

1. T. S. Eliot, *Four Quartets* (New York: Houghton Mifflin Harcourt, 2014), 59.
2. From our Israeli guide, Avishai!
3. Isaiah 11:6; Revelation 21:1–4
4. This story has been told in varying ways over the centuries; my telling is the sum total of them.